The Tourist's Guide to Las Vegas

An Inside Look at Sin City for visitors of all ages

*By: Adam & Cassy Laliberte

Forward

My husband and I fell in love with Las Vegas at different points in our lives. I was single and loved to travel to escape the hectic life of being a teacher! I also loved to travel here with my Mom, really as a fun girls trip.

My husband fell in love with Sin City as a single man, about to be married – to me! Our first trip together to Vegas was as an engaged couple in 2014. We got married at the Excalibur in April 2014, and have traveled there each year, since then. I guess you can say that I transferred my love of Vegas to my husband, who I knew would love the city as much as I always have!

We hope we can give you some valuable insights, hints, and tips on how to best enjoy this amazing place!

Thanks for reading!

-Adam & Cassy Laliberte

Dedication

We dedicate this book to my Mom, Susie Brouse, and to our niece and nephew, Hannah and Trevor! They continue to inspire us to write and to be creatively charged each day! Thank you!

-   *Adam & Cassy Laliberte*

Photo Credits

Table of Contents

Introduction

Introduction: Our Mission

Our mission is two-fold

* We want to help you plan for and have the most amazing trip you can possibly have!

* We also want you and your family to save money while still being able to see and do all that Las Vegas has to offer you!

Most guidebooks are simply full of information – some good and some irrelevant. Unlike a lot of guidebooks, we are biased, we admit - biased because we want to tell you what Las Vegas really has to offer so you have the most fun, efficient trip you can possibly have. We have been to Las Vegas many times, and consider ourselves very proficient and up-to-date on the city. This guide will help guide you, regardless of what group you happen to fall in, to have the most amazing time you can possibly have.

As this giant castle above may suggest, this is a city filled with fantasy, romance, and surprises. We are a married couple who got hitched in this castle above, the Chapel at Excalibur! We hold great memories of our many trips here, and want to make you, as our valued reader, aware and excited about the many possibilities that Vegas has to offer for every guest.

Las Vegas is, in our humble opinion, the ideal place to take a trip. The weather is almost perfect, as there is virtually no humidity, as it sits in the basin of the Mojave Desert, and beautiful mountains surround this vast city. There is a myriad of activities here for almost anyone to enjoy, making Las Vegas a very well-rounded city for visitors.

Chapter 1: Arriving & Orientation

Las Vegas is amazing now, and truly an oasis in the desert, but it did not used to look this way. In fact, it was not too long ago that it was literally a tiny town in the middle of stark Nevada desert. The city was officially incorporated as a city in 1911, and two decades later, as the Hoover Dam was built, in the 1930's, workers needed a fun place to go, and also to stay. Hotels were built, slowly turning this town into a true, touristy city. Today, Las Vegas is booming, and constantly growing and evolving.

The Mirage, built in 1989 by famed Vegas hotel owner Steve Wynn, was the first of the themed resorts, and truly started this now famed genre of thematic hotels. More hotels soon followed, and the city underwent a serious building boom for years, and continues to do so, especially with the relatively new, multi-billion - dollar City Center, complete amazing hotels, condos, and shopping. Today visitors can wander Vegas and tour realistic replications of cities like New York, Venice, and ancient Rome. Below is a quick visual reference to greater Las Vegas.

Greater Las Vegas area

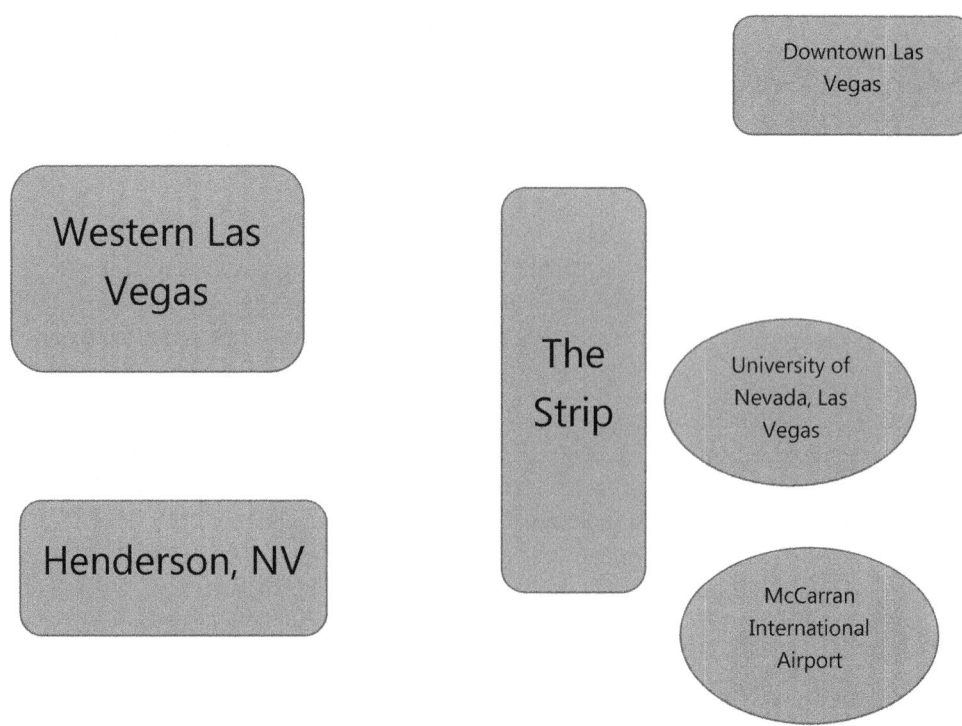

Much like Disney World and its' wildly popular thematic hotels, Las Vegas beckons guests not only with the fun of casinos, but with the very idea of being immersed in these themed giants. If you are a fan of Italy, as most of us are, head for Bellagio, The Venetian, or Caesars Palace. If city life is more your thing, go for New York, New York. Beach people should head for the Mirage or Mandalay Bay, with amazing pool and beach complexes. Get the idea? There's a resort for everyone in this town.

Fun fact! Did you know that almost 37 Million people travel to Las Vegas each year? This mecca in the dessert is one of the premier and most popular tourist destinations in the entire world.

Why the popularity? We think it's because Vegas has something for everyone. It is hard to imagine someone truly hating a place where you can swim, shop, go to a spa, get married, and play the slots – all in one day! Plus, the weather's perfect almost every month of the year. This is truly a 24/7 kind of town, so it will also appeal, of course, to the night owl in your party!

We hope you will find excitement in this book, as you prepare for your trip!

Arriving and Getting Situated

Get a lot of sleep before this flight, if you indeed are flying to Vegas. If you are driving to Sin City, also be sure to prepare for a drive that will take you into the desert. Make sure to stock up on bottled water, a first aid kit, a handy cell phone, and some snacks. Always confirm any hotel and airline reservations before you head out.

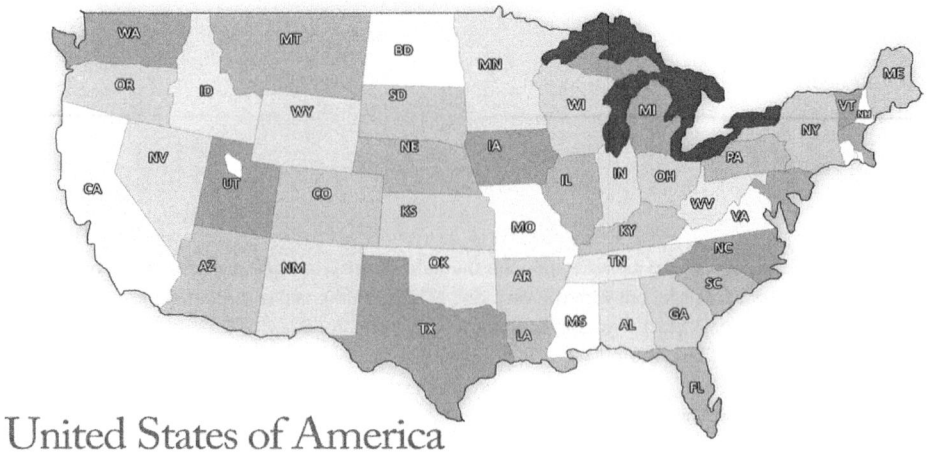

United States of America

As you fly in, after what, undoubtedly, may be a long, arduous flight, you will see the city pop up, almost out of nowhere. As you can see from the map above, Nevada is located in the southwestern part of the United States of America. Las Vegas, located in southern Nevada, is about a five-hour flight from most east coast cities. From Los Angeles, it is an easy one-hour flight.

If you're lucky enough to head to Vegas on a night flight, especially for your first visit, the view is unlike anything else in the world. All of a sudden, you gaze out of the windows and are rewarded with the vision of millions of sparkling lights adoring the massive hotels, stretched out before you. Las Vegas's great and easy to use airport, McCarran International, is only a few miles from the city, which makes the descent even that more spectacular. **The address is: 5757 Wayne Newton Blvd, Las Vegas, 89119. The phone number is: 1.702.261.5100.**

As you gather your bags, and your undoubtedly excitement builds, you will head into the airport and instantly see a row of slot machines. That's when you look at your companion with a knowing look. "Yes, honey, we are in Vegas!" The excitement builds as you walk further into the airport and see huge posters advertising all the current shows that Vegas is known for. Simply put, there are few places in the world that exude this kind of energy.

Getting to your hotel is easy.

Taxis vs. Bell Trans

Taxis are plentiful, but can be

a poor value, compared to the

far cheaper Bell Transportation.

(See the hot tip.)

If you are arriving at an off-time, such as

late at night, or early in the morning,

it can definitely be cheaper and

less stressful to take a taxi than

a shared shuttle, like Bell Trans.

These shuttles can be found at Terminal 1, outside door 9, and also at Terminal 3, outside door 52.

> ## Hot Tip!
>
> The number for Bell Trans is: 702.736.4428. and the website is: www.airportshuttlelasvegas.com. This is your best bet for value, coming and going to the airport.

A taxi from the airport will set you back anywhere from $10 to $25, depending on what hotel you are staying at. Downtown hotels are more expensive to travel to, as they are slightly further from the airport than the Strip hotels.

If you are arriving at a peak time, it will be better to take Bell Trans, as the taxi fare can be expensive sitting in traffic. If you simply don't care about money or just want to get to your hotel quickly, take the taxi. In our experience, cabbies in Las Vegas are generally kind and hospitable.

All hotels in Vegas and surrounding Henderson are a quick drive from the airport, making Vegas one of the most convenient places in America to fly directly into. You may have a wait to board a Bell Transportation shared shuttle, but the lower cost and peace of mind, however, may be worth it.

Once you arrive at your hotel, there will likely be a very short to moderate wait, as most hotels have a thriving front desk that caters to their guests.

Arrival at your resort

Arriving at a Las Vegas hotel, especially for a Vegas virgin, is a very unique experience. Whether it is twelve noon or four am, the casino will be hopping, at least moderately, and there will be at least one eatery open. Most hotels will check in guests at around three pm, but often you can get into your room earlier. Check-out time is usually eleven am or noon, and late check-out is often available for a small fee.

When we arrived a little after midnight, we were still able to order a great meal at a restaurant to take back to our room. There is nothing like noshing on a cheeseburger and fries in the middle of the night, knowing you will wake up the next morning to tackle Vegas!

Chapter 2 - Tours & Sample Itineraries

A common question that visitors have is where to start? The city is not overwhelmingly large, but there are many different ways to tackle it, and many visitors are confused as to where to begin exploring this exciting city. You can wander around, and not really have a game plan, or you be a bit more organized, and take time to really have a fun itinerary that will maximize your time in Vegas.

City & Surrounding Area Tours

Some visitors will opt to explore the city and surroundings on their own, and many will want a fully-guided tour. We personally enjoy both, as it's nice to venture out on our own, but also a tour will give you that personal touch and expertise that going out on your own does not offer you. The following two websites, along with this guidebook, will explain the many tours that Vegas offers.

www.tripadvisor.com

Warning! We will discuss this amazing website several times in this book, because this site is the Bible of the travel industry. The world's largest and most comprehensive travel website, tripadvisor.com will give you detailed, up-to-date reviews and prices on attractions that Vegas offers, as well as hotels and restaurants.

We love the photos that the attractions/hotels add to this website, as well as visitor photos, which are most helpful. What could be more useful than real reviews, from real travelers? This website is a quick way to let you know if that attraction, restaurant, or hotel that you want is a dud or a winner.

www.vegas.com.

1.866.983.4279

This is a jewel of a website, and it serves as a great companion to this guidebook. From bus tours to helicopter tours to seeing the Grand Canyon, this website allows you to browse each tour and book it right here online, as well. Detailed information on each attraction in Vegas is also displayed very succinctly.

Our favorite Vegas tours

Each of the following tours can be booked online, at **www.tripadvisor.com**, and through a company called **Grayline Tours** (1.800.472.9546.) or through **www.vegas.com**. (1.866.983.4279). The following tours are the best of the best, in our opinion. Please check the websites we listed for current prices and lengths of these tours, as they do change constantly.

Recommended Tours

- Shopping tours that visit several hot shopping stops
- Nightlife tours that visit 3 or 4 hot spots in one night (bars/nightclubs)
- Hop-on, hop-off tours through Las Vegas
- Horseback rides through the desert

Deuce Bus

The Deuce bus is a great option for all travelers to Vegas. It is a double-decker bus that runs, 24 hours a day, from the a few miles beyond Mandalay Bay, at the southern end of the Strip, all the way to the downtown area. Stops are plentiful, and located outside most hotels on the Strip and at the Fremont Experience in the downtown area. There are several other stops in the downtown area, as well. You can buy a 24-hour, all-day pass for $8, and also multi-day passes, as well. Check out: **www.rtcsnv.com** for detailed and up-to-date schedules.

Monorail Service

Ten years ago, there was no major monorail service in Vegas, only smaller ones. Well, today there are monorails that really help visitors shuttle from place to place, and trust us, when it's 105 degrees outside, these will come in very handy!

*Monorail # 1 is the major monorail in Vegas, and the only one that is not complimentary. It runs from the MGM Grand all the way to the Las Vegas Convention Center, and then on to the nearby SLS hotel, formerly known as the Sahara. Please note that this monorail does not take visitors downtown. The cost for an all-day pass is $12, and a one-time pass is $5. Multi-day passes are also available. This runs from 7 am to midnight on Mondays, from 7 am to 2 am Tuesday through Thursdays, and from 7 am until 3 am Fridays through Sunday.

*Monorail #2 transports guests from Mandalay Bay to the Luxor and then onto the Excalibur. Catch this at either of the hotels. This runs daily from 9 am until 10:30 pm.

*Monorail #3 shuttles guests from the Monte Carlo, then to Aria in City Center, and finally onto the Bellagio. You can catch this monorail at either of the three hotels. This monorail runs daily from 8 am to 4 am.

*Monorail #4 runs from the Mirage to Treasure Island, and this is the quickest monorail ride in town, but it still offers great views of Las Vegas and both resorts. This runs from 7 am to 4 am, daily.

Itineraries to Pursue

Depending on what category you fall into, your itinerary will, of course, differ. As a basic rule of thumb, no matter where you are staying, you will most likely want to spend at least two full days on the world-famous Strip. Home to jaw-dropping themed hotels like Excalibur and the Mirage, a visitor could easily spend at least four or five days here – shopping, gorging at the lavish buffets, visiting the attractions, and seeing the shows.

Here are some of our favorite itineraries! Note, too, that all three focus on the Strip. If you choose to stay off strip at a hotel like Hard Rock, Rio, or Sam's Town, simply take a shuttle (which most have), or a taxi to the Strip, and then start these itineraries.

Sample Itinerary: Young Singles & Couples

* Go ahead - sleep in a little, or a lot! After all, you are on vacation. Try a **breakfast buffet**, which is always cheaper than a lunch or dinner buffet. You should ideally spend your first day on the Strip, and this itinerary focuses on the Strip itself.

* After filling up, walk the Strip, and check out this amazing stretch of architectural wonders. Stop and **shop** at the Forum Shops at Caesars Palace, or the Grand Canal Shoppes at the Venetian. These by far are the two most themed and elegant shopping malls on the Strip. Allow an hour or two to shop.

*For a **tasty lunch**, try the fabulous restaurant, Stripside Cafe, which is outside Caesars, and almost on the Strip itself. Mon Ami Gabi at Paris also features amazing outdoor seating and an upscale but not pretentious dining atmosphere. A **buffet** is always cheaper at lunch than at dinner, so you can save serious money by having a lunch buffet, then having a smaller dinner.

*After lunch, **explore** the mid-Strip hotels, like the elegant Bellagio, and try to catch its' light show. After ogling the fountains, hit the Monte Carlo, which can be easily reached via monorail from the Bellagio. On the way, stop at Crystals shopping center in the Aria. It is located on thesame monorail line. The trip itself is fun, as waiting for the monorail gives you a nice birds eye view of Vegas.

*After doing some serious monorail hopping, **play some slots** at some Mid-strip hotels. The Excalibur, Luxor, and Mandalay Bay are easily reached by a tram that connects all three. Each hotel is a hoot, and we recommend stopping also at New York, New York, and wandering around this perfect recreation of Manhattan. The casino here is fun and action-packed.

*For dinner,** we recommend a buffet or, if you are on a strict budget, aim for a food court or your hotel's coffee shop.

*Night beckons, and you definitely need to **hit a show**. We recommend Criss Angel's new show, Mindfreak Live, at Luxor. If you are a magic fan, this is the show and the magician to spend your money on. If you want more variety, choose a Cirque show (there are many!), or Terry Fator, an amazing ventriloquist and singer.

Itinerary for Families with Kids

*For **breakfast,** it is always easy to either hit a buffet or grab a quick nosh at your hotel. Most kid- oriented hotels, such as Circus Circus, have a Krispy Kreme or a McDonalds, where you can grab a quick and cheap breakfast.

*Spend some time at **Circus Circus**, at the Adventuredome, the country's largest indoor amusement park. Most rides here, are, no surprise, very kid-friendly, but there are a few rides and roller coasters that pack a serious punch for older kids and parents. The **Secret Garden at the Mirage** is also amazing, and very educational and fun for all ages.

*A **buffet** is a great option for kids. A great, cheaper option is the buffet at Excalibur. The very efficient double-decker city bus, the Deuce, will get you and your family there easily. Take a few minutes after dinner to explore the **Fun Dungeon** arcade beneath Excalibur's giant casino.

*In the afternoon, we recommend **Gregory Popovich** or **Nathan Burton's Comedy Magic show**. Also, **Mac King** at Harrah's, is great with kids. These shows are kid-pleasers, and are a great way to also kill a few hours if the kids are getting bored.

*For **dinner**, head back to your hotel and regroup. Catch a quick dinner there at a coffee shop or a pizza place. Nighttime is a perfect time in Vegas **hit the pool**, and have some fun downtime. Whew. What a day. Rest up for another day of family (we hope) fun!

Itinerary for Older Couples & Singles

*For **breakfast**, try a coffee shop at your hotel or a breakfast buffet. A great buffet can be had at the Mirage's Cravings buffet (more expensive) or Luxor (less expensive and a good bang for your buck.)

*After gorging at breakfast, simply **wander the Strip for awhile, and soak up the atmosphere**. If you have difficulty walking, there is a great city bus, the Deuce, that will take you, rather cheaply, up and down the Strip for the day. Bus stops are conveniently located outside most hotels. Taxis are also located outside each hotel, and are not too expensive.

*For lunch, consider a buffet when the prices are lower**. These are always cheaper at lunch than at dinner, and almost every hotel has a great buffet. If you find yourself mid-Strip, try **Mirage's Cravings buffet**. A great value is had at **Sam's Town's Firelight Buffet**, which is a quick, free bus ride via Harrah's casino.

*A fun thing for seniors and older couples is to **try the slots or a table game**. Roulette is also a fun and easy game to play. Most dealers are very friendly, but if you are uncomfortable, try a table that is empty to alleviate any embarrassement that may pop up.

*For dinner, try a nice sit-down restaurant at your hotel**. All hotels have moderate and expensive eateries, and most have food courts if you want to save some money.

*A show** is always exciting at night, and there are many different options to choose from. If you are into magic, we suggest David Copperfield for seniors. The Mirage's Terry Fator is amazing.

Chapter 3 – Accommodations

Fun fact!

There are nearly 125,000 hotel rooms in Vegas, placing Las Vegas in the top 3 cities in the country for most hotel rooms. Rest assured, you will not have trouble finding a hotel.

Do you know that Las Vegas has the most AAA five-diamond hotels of any city in the world? So, of course, one of the first questions anyone asks themselves before heading to Sin City, is "Where should I stay?" There are so many options to choose from, from huge, gaudy show-stoppers to immaculately themed hotels, such as the famed Venetian Hotel. **We recommend, especially for your first trip, a themed hotel, such as Luxor or the Venetian.** You could roll the dice and stay at a Best Western or a Marriott, which are great options, but to really feel the soul and spirit that is Vegas, go for an over-the-top themed hotel and casino.

Did you also know that 17 of the 20 largest hotels in the world are in Las Vegas?

Hotels we cover will come in five categories: Strip, Downtown, West of the Strip, East of the Strip, and off the Strip.

The Strip

This is where the real action is. For a first-time visitor, especially, this is probably where you will want to spend most of your vacation. There is a ton of amazing shopping and dining choices here, and resorts include the Bellagio, Venetian, Luxor, and Mirage.

Downtown

North of the Strip is a very different Las Vegas – the downtown area. This is home to legendary hotels like the Four Queens, the Golden Nugget, and Main Street Station. This area is more adult-oriented and may not appeal to everyone. Hotels tend to be less expensive here, as well.

East of the Strip

The East of the Strip is a great location for travelers who want a more relaxed, less hectic atmosphere. Popular hotels here include the Hard Rock Hotel and Casino, and the all-suite Platinum Hotel. UNLV is nearby, and McCarran airport is conveniently located here, as well. Many hotels here are a quick walk from the Strip.

West of the Strip

Hotels west of the Strip include the famed party-central Rio Hotel and Casino. It is easy to find a hotel, like the Rio, or the similarly young and hip Palms here that offers free shuttle service to the Strip. Other great hotels include the fun Orleans hotel.

Hotels Way off the Strip

You certainly don't need to stay on the Las Vegas Strip to have a good time in Vegas, but it is more convenient. Hotels in nearby Henderson can be a great value, however, and include Hilton Lake Las Vegas. Sam's Town, which is in the city of Las Vegas itself and a quick drive away, is a winner, and a local favorite.

Where should we stay?

This is, perhaps, the most common question visitors ask themselves when they think of Vegas. The choices are almost overwhelming. Here is a quick reference guide that will help get you to "your" hotel.

For....

Animal Lovers – Flamingo, Mandalay Bay, Mirage

Beach people – Mandalay Bay, Mirage, Tropicana

Casino lovers – Bellagio, MGM Grand, Monte Carlo, Paris, Wynn

Elegance without too much sticker shock – MGM Grand, Mirage, Paris, Treasure Island

Foodies – Bellagio, Caesars, Paris, Venetian, Wynn

Off-the- Strip decadence – Golden Nugget, Plaza

Off-the-Strip value – California, Gold Coast, Golden Nugget, Main Street Station, Orleans, Sam's Town

On the Strip Value – Circus Circus, Excalibur, Harrah's, Luxor, Stratosphere

Non-casino value – Hilton Lake Las Vegas, Platinum, Trump Las Vegas

Party-Goers - Hard Rock, Palms, Planet Hollywood, Rio

Pure Decadence – Aria, Cosmopolitan, Bellagio, Encore, Mandarin Oriental, Palazzo, Trump, Venetian, Wynn

Shoppers – Bellagio, Caesars, Planet Hollywood, Venetian

Spa enthusiasts – Aria, Bellagio, Caesars, Venetian

Thrill Seekers – Circus Circus, New York, New York, Stratosphere

Money-saving tips

A huge question and consideration when booking any Vegas trip, or any trip in general, of course, is money and your budget. It's always a good idea to have an overall budget, and remember that most times, you will end up spending more.

Keep in mind little things, like forgotten supplies, such as sunscreen, tips for bellmen and taxi drivers, and snacks, such as gelato and candy. All of these items will add expenses to your budget, so try to factor them in when coming up with an overall trip budget.

Here are some tips we have learned over the years that will help you get the best deal and save money on your trip!

- **Call the hotel directly and bargain**. If you see that Harrah's, for instance, is going for $59 a night, ask the manager for $40 a night. It never hurts to bargain, but be polite and persistent. Remember – the whole point of a hotel or a resort is to sell the room, and management will often reduce the room rather than leave it empty and not earn a dime.

- **Always try to travel during the week, if you can**. If we can, we always head to Vegas on a Sunday and stay for at least five days. Rates are almost always cheaper Sundays through Thursdays, and then go up on the weekends, as the demand is higher for rooms on those days. When the demand is up, rates go up, as well, so plan for this.

- We really love the website **www.booking.com**, as it is easy to go back and change your plans and also to re-book your trip if the price goes down. Sometimes on this website, which offers low prices, you can also pay when you get there, and reserve your room only with a credit or debit card. You can also cancel almost any trip for free, which is an added bonus.

- **Make sure to factor in the hotel's dreaded resort fee** when budgeting for your trip, which can be as much as $40 a night! Some hotels downtown and off the Strip do not have one, but all hotels on the Strip have one. Yes, they pay for some items, such as local calls and bottled water, but many are just a way for hotels to advertise cheap rates, which are not quite as cheap as they appear!

- It can be beneficial to bid for a hotel on **www.priceline.com.** We aren't always a fan, and beware of resort fees when using priceline. As a general rule of thumb, priceline will tell you what the median price of the hotel(s) you are seeking, and you can bid accordingly. If the hotel you want has a median price of $100, for example, try bidding at least $65. If you bid too low, priceline will reject your bid. **www.biddingfortravel.com** is a great website that lists most of the hotels that are on the priceline website.

- **Priceline also has some great express deals, which are rooms that have not been sold, and these can be a great deal, especially if you book at the last minute.**

- **We have just discovered that MGM Resorts allows guests, in most cases, to be on a payment plan for their vacations**. If the deposit falls within their guidelines, you automatically quality for a payment plan, which can help you not necessarily save money, but this may help you to set aside money each month for your trip, which we love to do. Head to: **www.mgmresortvacations.com** for more details.

Map of the Strip

(* = the Strip, also known as Las Vegas Boulevard)

Stratosphere   *

Circus Circus   *

Fashion Show Mall &
Trump Las Vegas   *   Wynn & Encore

Treasure Island   *

Mirage   *   Venetian

                                *   Harrah's
Caesar's Palace   *   Cromwell, Flamingo

Bellagio & City Center   *   Bally's, Paris
                                *

Monte Carlo   *   Planet Hollywood

New York, New York   *   MGM Grand

Excalibur   *   Tropicana

Luxor   *

Mandalay Bay   *

South Strip

Featured Hotel : Luxor – South Strip

www.luxor.com. 702.262.4000. 2900 Las Vegas Blvd. South. 4,400 units. $59 and up. Daily resort fee: $30.

This giant, black, pyramid-shaped hotel is simply a feast for the senses. We are biased, of course, because your lovely authors stayed in a suite here during our 2014 marriage at the Excalibur. The theme here is, of course, Egypt. In recent years, the theme has been toned down considerably, and now shows up primarily in the great, affordable buffet, and, of course, in the hotel's pyramid design. The hotel is striking, and thousands of visitors each day stop and take photo after photo of this architectural wonder.

Inside, the atrium is described as the world's largest, and you can almost fall over as you stare up at the vastness. It is truly a dizzying effect on the senses. Luxor has over 4,000 well-maintained and beautiful guest rooms, making it one of the largest in Vegas, and in the world, in fact.

A majority of these rooms overlook the atrium, and it is a very cool thing to step out of your hotel room and stare down at the mass of humanity, restaurants, and shops below. The other rooms and suites are located in two adjacent towers, and these rooms are less-themed but still very nice. The staff we have encountered here has always been friendly and gracious.

One of the perks of staying at the Luxor is that is its' close proximity to other hotels. Mandalay Bay and Excalibur are both directly accessible by a monorail, with Luxor being a middle stop on this fun train ride. There is also a quick, moveable walkway to Excalibur, and it is also an easy walk in the other direction to Mandalay Bay. New York, New York, MGM Grand, and the Tropicana are all a quick five to ten-minute stroll away.

The Luxor also boasts a beautifully-landscaped pool area, with jaw-dropping views of the Luxor itself, as well as the beautiful mountains.

Other Recommended South Strip Hotels

Excalibur

www.excalibur.com. 702.597.7700. 3850 Las Vegas Blvd. South. 4,008 units. $29 and up. Daily resort fee: $30.

The Excalibur is a giant castle of a hotel that sports an amazing medieval theme. We got married here, at the Chapel at Excalibur, and simply love this hotel. The Excalibur is a very family-friendly resort that is also very affordable. It is not uncommon to see rates as low as $29 here, and the rooms are very nice. The Tower rooms are fairly basic, and feature older amenities, but the Contemporary rooms are upgraded and feature nice marble-topped vanities and larger flat-screen tvs.

The Medieval village of the Excalibur connects directly with the Luxor, and features a winding pathway of restaurants, fast-food outlets, and cute souvenir shops. There is a great selection of food here, with a well-stocked food court and great restaurants, including the affordable and tasty buffet. There is a spacious arcade area underneath the casino called The Dungeon, which kids will go crazy for, as well as a nice but pretty basic pool complex.

Mandarin Oriental

www.mandarinoriental.com/lasvegas. 1.702.590.8888. 3752 Las Vegas Blvd. South. 392 units. $199 and up. Daily resort fee: $39.

A true 5-star stunner, the Mandarin Oriental brand is known world-wide for its class, elegance, and stunning rooms and service. It is consistently rated as one of the top two resorts in Las Vegas, and is located perfectly at City Center, in the center of the thriving Strip. A nice monorail at Aria, located next-door, connects guests quickly to the Bellagio and Monte Carlo.

When entering the resort, guests are whisked up to the elegant 23rd floor Sky lobby for check-in. Views of the Strip from this lobby are, of course, amazing, and really set the scene for your stay here. Rooms are very upscale, and be prepared for leather furnishings, flatscreen tvs, and lots of marble. Two-hundred residential units are also here, so if you really like it, hey – you can think about living here, right?

A two-story spa and salon is one of the best in town, and the Mandarin Oriental also features yoga and a very nice pool area. Very comfy chaise lounges, a posh pool café, and views of the Strip, the other City Center hotels, and the mountains are priceless. A French restaurant and the Mandarin Bar are two other dining options. This is a hotel option for upscale travelers, provided you are OK with not having a casino downstairs, of course.

Mandalay Bay

www.mandalaybay.com. 1.877.632.7800. 3,950 Las Vegas Blvd South. $99 and up. Daily resort fee: $35.

This is a 5-star stunner that has a Polynesian theme, but lacks a prime location on the Strip. This hotel is elegant without being too stuffy, however, which will appeal to most visitors. The feel here is of a luxury hotel, and the resort received a much-needed upgrade in 2013.

The beach and pool area is expansive, and is a huge draw for this massive hotel and resort. This attraction features slides, a massive sandy beach, and a lazy river – a big draw for kids and adults alike. Mandalay Bay also offers the Shark Reef attraction, which is a pricey but fun attraction that families seem to love.

The hotel also features elegantly appointed guest rooms with lots of amenities like marble vanities, and large windows overlooking either the mountains or the Strip. Mandalay Bay, while situated at the very end of the south Strip, is, however, conveniently located on the monorail that connects it to the Luxor and then on to the Excalibur.

You will not lack for great places to eat, drink, or shop here, that's for sure. Mandalay Bay features over ten places to eat, including the obligatory buffet (pricey). The resort also features a nice shopping arcade with unique shops, that connects with the Luxor.

You will pay to stay here, that's for sure, but room rates rarely raise above a hundred bucks, which is a steal for any 5-star Vegas resort.

MGM Grand

www.mgmgrand.com. 702.891.7777. 3799 Las Vegas Blvd. South. 5,034 units. Daily resort fee: $35.

One of the largest hotels in the world, and the largest in Vegas, in terms of room numbers, the MGM Grand is a massive green giant. The resort occupies a prime location across from New York, New York, and next to Planet Hollywood.

Over twenty amazing dining options are here, including the Rainforest Café, which is a treat for adults and kids alike. MGM's buffet is a bit pricey, but features a wide medley of tasty options, including many different and unique stations and a fully-stocked dessert selection. Joel Robuchon, the famed, much Michelin-starred French chef, has not one but two! restaurants here, adding a major touch of class to this resort.

The famous lion habitat, which used to be smack dab in the middle of the giant casino, is, alas, no longer there, but visitors can head to a ranch in Vegas to see the famous tigers. A giant shopping arcade and one of the largest casinos in Vegas are also big draws.

What makes the MGM Grand even more convenient is a handy stop on the Monorail, and great entertainment options, including award-winning illusionist David Copperfield. Cirque du Soleil's KA, which is always a good bet, is also a headliner here. The pool area, one of the best in Vegas, is also a big draw, complete with a lazy river and multiple, luxuriously-landscaped pools.

New York, New York

www.nynyhotelcasino.com. 702.740.6969. 3790 Las Vegas Blvd. South. 2,024 units. $69 and up. Daily resort fee: $35.

Many residents of Manhattan like to call their city the best in the world, and we personally love this bustling, exciting city. A near perfect recreation of the Big Apple, New York, New York is a fun place to stay or simply visit for a few hours. This place definitely evokes the real Manhattan.

Winding streets inside simulate the famous Greenwich Village, with a wide array of dining and shopping options. A very convenient, casual cluster of eateries, including a deli and authentic New York style pizza shop, are always bustling. A giant shop, Hershey World, located right inside the resort, on the ground floor, is a must for the kids, with dozens of mouthwatering candies to choose from.

You can even stroll across a perfect, albeit much smaller recreation of the Brooklyn Bridge, right out front of this fun resort. There is also a thrilling roller coaster for the adrenaline junkie in your family, which we detail in our chapter for kids, and also in our thrills chapter.

New York, New York seems huge, but in reality it's one of the smallest resorts room-wise, with just over 2,000 units. We have heard that it can be a challenge to actually find your room once inside, but the rooms are nicely decorated, and are nicely appointed and also affordable.

Honorable Mention: South Strip - Monte Carlo

www.montecarlo.com. 702.730.7777. 3770 Las Vegas Blvd. South. 3,002 units. $69 and up. Daily resort fee: $30.

The Monte Carlo is an often overlooked hotel that is, to us, simply magical. It occupies a prime location next to City Center, with its' hotels and shops, and also stands next to the excitement of New York, New York. Monte Carlo is also just a pretty hotel, evoking the glamour of the country of Monte Carlo. Statues and fountains abound as you enter this mellow, but, elegant hotel.

Personally, this was the first Las Vegas hotel that we ever stayed at, so naturally we have had a soft spot for it ever since then. There is an amazing smell that permeates this hotel – dare I say vanilla? And, yes, besides the smell, it has amazing amenities. Lush rooms are nice and spacious, but not too fancy or ritzy, which makes the price nice and affordable.

A smaller, boutique hotel, called Hotel 32, is actually located inside the Monte Carlo, on the top floor of this massive resort. A free limo ride from the airport whisks you to the entrance of the Monte Carlo, and you are greeted and taken to the lobby of Hotel 32. A very convenient club room with snacks is one of the highlights of this small, all-suite hotel. Prices here, are of course, steep, at around $150 or so a night, but the room furnishings and amenities makes it worth it to many.

A nice amenity that the Monte Carlo boasts is the monorail that directly links it to City Center's Aria hotel and shopping center, and then on to Bellagio. This means that any time of the day, especially at night, when you just want to quickly pop over to the Bellagio or City Center, for some shopping or gambling, you are a fun and quick monorail ride away.

Eateries to focus on here include Diablo's, a feisty, adult-oriented Mexican joint, right on the Strip, a nice buffet, and a convenient food court. The Monte Carlo also boasts a small shopping street with some handy retail stores. We feel that you can't go wrong here, especially if this is your first trip to Las Vegas.

Center Strip

The Center Strip is loosely defined as running from the Bellagio to Treasure Island. This is a particularly upscale part of Vegas, which you will see very quickly, as you explore these massive resorts. From the striking architecture of the Bellagio to the iconic Mirage resort, Las Vegas Boulevard, replete with these amazing hotels, is a sight to behold.

Cromwell

www.caesars.com. 1.877.459.4292.3595 Las Vegas Blvd. South. 188 units. $159 and up. Daily resort fee: $35.

The Cromwell is a boutique hotel that many people easily overlook. It is a gem, however, that deserves a second glance. Situated ideally in the center of the Strip, right next to the Linq's really fun outdoor shopping plaza, the Cromwell boasts sumptuous rooms with 55-inch flatscreen tvs, leather headboards, and hardwood floors. A very hip and spacious pool area, and a casino tinted in red are just some of the amenities this boutique hotel offers.

A new restaurant boasting Italian food with California influences, Giada, by celebrity chef Giada DeLaurentiis, is a big hit here. Drai's, a humongous, 65,000 square foot indoor/outdoor pool and nightclub, is also very popular with guests and Vegas visitors. Check out this for a different Vegas experience.

Center Strip Featured Hotel: Mirage

www.mirage.com. 702.791.7111. 3400 Las Vegas Blvd. South. 3,044 units. $79 and up. Daily resort fee: $35

The Mirage, created by the famous Vegas visionary Steve Wynn, opened in 1989, as the first major themed hotel in Las Vegas. The mega-resort truly ushered in the whole thematic concept that now defines Vegas. The Mirage is cool, tropical, and hip, and one of those hotels that caters to every demographic. It can be cheap enough to make it affordable for most. Families, singles, and young couples all love this hotel, and seniors also love the mellow pool complex and perfect location – smack dab in the middle of all the Strip action.

A host of great restaurants and a nice, modern buffet, along with a host of fun shops help make the Mirage a fun place to stay. As you check-in to the hotel, a huge aquarium greets you, and the thousands of soothing plants and foliage truly makes guests feel like they are in a tropical destination.

Rooms are shiny and modern, with plush bathrooms and beds. Massive windows overlook either the mountains, the pool area, or the bustling Strip. You cannot go wrong with either view, really.

Try the buffet, which is very sleek and shiny in décor, and also the many affordable eateries including the venerable Carnegie Deli, an ice cream shop, and a bakery.

The pool area is amazing, with waterfalls, grottos, and bridges. It is a nice way to spend a few hours, or maybe even the whole day, but don't forget the sunscreen, as the Vegas sun can be brutal!

Terry Fator, the winner of America's Got Talent, is the major headliner here, and he is fabulous, bringing his world-class ventriloquist and singing skills to the stage. This is a funny show by a very talented man.

The Mirage really does have it all – a self-contained resort that is centrally located with tons ofamenities and restaurants. It's truly hard to go wrong here, especially if this is your first trip to Vegas.

Other Recommended Center Strip Hotels

Aria

www.aria.com. 1.702.590.7757. 3730 Las Vegas Blvd. South. 4,004 units. $159 and up. Daily resort fee: $39.

A swanky, five-star City Center stunner, the Aria also features a high-end shopping area called Crystals. This hotel is on a monorail line that connects it to Bellagio and Monte Carlo, and also boasts a nice pool area with sweeping views of the mountains and surrounding hotels. This is a top choice for travelers who don't mind spending some money to stay here, and for those who value a very central location.

Rooms are very modern in design, and feature floor-to-ceiling windows that offer amazing views of either the Strip or the towering mountains. Bathrooms are large and have lots of marble and frosted glass. Luxury is the word here, and Aria does this very well!

Part of the City Center mega-resort collection, with a prime center-Strip location, Aria sits next to the Bellagio on one side and flanks Monte Carlo on the other. As we mentioned, a very handy monorail connects it to these neighboring hotels, and helps make your trip more stress-free.

Top Pick – Bellagio

www.bellagio.com. 1.702.693.7111. 3600 Las Vegas Blvd. South. 3,933 units. $169 and up. Daily resort fee: $39.

Truly one of the world's most sumptuous and beautiful resorts, the Bellagio is located smack dab in the middle of the Strip. Flanking the City Center hotels and Caesars Palace, the location here simply can't be beat if you want to be mid-Strip.

Like Aria and Caesars Palace, the Bellagio is a fairly pricey hotel, but you get major bang for your buck here. The casino exudes elegance, and the pool area is spacious, posh, and very European. A 40,000 - square - foot spa caters to guests with a myriad of services, as well, just daring you to be truly pampered. Fourteen restaurants, both casual and swank, a high-end shopping area, and a beautiful conservatory and outdoor fountains make the Bellagio a truly self-contained resort.

Rooms are very tastefully done up in shades of ivory, brown, and maroon, and feature stunning marble-topped vanities. The feel is very five-star, and very chic. The higher your room, of course, the better the view you have, and we encourage guests to try and snag a room overlooking the fountains – the sight of the dancing waters, from your very own room, is a sight to behold, and truly a unique hotel experience.

The Bellagio Buffet is one of the priciest in town, but is a great value. Set in a modern and expansive space, the buffet offers wood-fired pizzas, many fresh stations, and a dizzying array of tantalizing desserts.

An added bonus of staying at the Bellagio is the handy monorail that connects this resort to both Aria at the City Center resorts and also to the Monte Carlo. It is a very convenient way, especially at night, to travel around the Strip. Right next door is also Caesars Palace, where you can shop till you drop at the fabulous Forum Shops.

Top Pick - Caesars Palace

www.caesarspalace.com. 1.702.731.7710. 3570 Las Vegas Boulevard South. 3,960 units. $129 and up. Daily resort fee: $35.

One of our top picks in Vegas, Caesars was built in 1966, and remains to this day one of the most beautiful resorts in town. It is a bit over the top, with Roman columns and accents that adorn the rooms, but it is very four-star experience. Guests often receive a glass of champagne during their wait in line to check-in – yes, it's that kind of resort!

Caesars also boasts a dizzying array of restaurants and a shopping mall, the Forum Shops, that is the most successful in the nation. All this – downstairs, and just a short walk from your room!

The pool complex, aptly named the Garden of the Gods, is infamous in Vegas, with 8 pools that are European in elegance, and downright a pleasure to spend a day in.

The Stripside Café is a cool and hip new eatery option right on the Strip, with tasty desserts, and menu items like onion rings, burgers and shakes. Caesars is notorious for being very expensive with its' room rates and food prices, but what you get for the money is amazingly worth it. The location alone is smack dab in the center of the Strip, and very amenable to walking to most major hotels.

Paris Las Vegas Casino Resort

www.parislv.com. 1.702.946.7000. 3655 Las Vegas Boulevard South. 2,916 units. $119 and up. Daily resort fee: $35.

If you love the City of Light, like we do, you will probably love this very elegant hotel smack dab in the middle of the Strip. Across the street is the Bellagio, a five-minute walk away, and connected to Bally's, Paris is ideally situated, and offers a great, French-feeling buffet and cute little shops and quaint restaurants.

Rooms here are very nice, with lots of marble and large, sumptuous bathrooms. They are not cheap, for sure, but they are a good value, however, if you want a perfect location and a beautiful hotel. On a side note, the casino has always been one of our favorites, and there is even a faux Eiffel Tower you can ride to the top of, just like the real Paris! *Ooh la la!*

The Eiffel Tower experience is a nice amenity that Paris offers, as you can pay to ascend to the top of the faux Eiffel Tower, with its' amazing views of the Bellagio and its' fountains. An elegantly landscaped pool area with chaise lounges and cabanas is also a reason to book a room at Paris.

Planet Hollywood

www.planethollywoodresort.com. 1.702.785.5555. 3667 Las Vegas Blvd. South. 3,768 units. $89 and up. Daily resort fee: $35.

Yes, there is a huge Planet Hollywood smack dab in the center of the Strip, and it's a very nice hotel. Situated between Paris and the Showcase Mall and the MGM Grand, this hotel may appealmost to movie fans and the younger set, with special movie memorabilia in each beautifully appointed room.

Formerly known as the Aladdin, which we do miss, Planet Hollywood has nonetheless morphed into a nice hotel that boasts a perfect location. Almost outside your front door is the gleaming Bellagio across the street, and the fabulous Caesar's Palace and their Forum Shops are also smack dab across the street, giving Planet Hollywood a perfect location.

A nice, albeit tame pool complex, with two pools and two Jacuzzis, and tasty eateries like the Sugar Factory and Gordon Ramsey's delicious restaurant, BurGR, are just some of the amenities this hotel has to offer.

The atmospheric Miracle Mile shopping complex, with a plethora of hip shops and eateries, is a bonus. Britney Spears and the Backstreet Boys are two of the headliners here, and magic acts like the fabulous Nathan Burton allow this resort to boast about their variety of talent.

If you are into the movies, and want a resort with a prime, central Strip, location, you can't go wrong here.

North Strip hotels

We define North Strip hotels as those that run from Harrah's to the Stratosphere. The term "North Strip" is fairly subjective, but for the purposes of this book, we will assume that the North Strip begins at Harrah's.

Circus Circus

www.circuscircus.com. 1.702. 734. 0410. 2880 Las Vegas Blvd. South. 3,774 units. $20 and up. Daily resort fee: $27.

A sprawling kid-favorite, Circus Circus is a bit loud, chaotic, and definitely features loads of family fun! Featuring the largest indoor amusement park in the country, the Adventuredome, Circus Circus has over 3,700 rooms in three different towers, and even a fun aerial tram that connects the towers. A permanent circus is also featured here (hence the name: Circus Circus), and this circus is very talented, drawing international performers sure to please your little ones.

The best thing about this hotel? Rates go as low as $20 a night for the least-expensive rooms here, the Manor rooms, which are located in a separate building These rooms used to be very unappealing, but have recently been renovated, and are in much better shape now. Guests routinely report that the rooms in the main three towers also boast nice amenities such as granite countertops and colorful furnishings.

Circus Circus has numerous restaurants, including an affordable and good buffet, a Krispy Kreme, a pizzeria, and a very good steakhouse, aptly named The Steakhouse. An attractive shopping arcade is right outside the Adventuredome, and two expansive pools round out the must-see amenities of this giant hotel.

The location of Circus Circus leaves a bit to be desired, as it is a good ten-minute walk from the Venetian (which isn't too bad), but we don't think this makes a huge difference, especially if you enjoy a nice walk. The Wynn is about a ten-minute walk away. Of course, the handy Deuce bus is right outside the hotel, waiting to whisk you up and down the Strip.

Harrahs

www.harrahslasvegas.com. 1.702.369.5000. 3475 Las Vegas Blvd. South. 2,526 units. $69 and up. Daily resort fee: $30.

An American classic, Harrah's is a very Vegasy hotel. What does that mean for the traveler? A huge, sprawling casino, a decent buffet, and a nice shopping arcade. Over 2,500 rooms are nicely-appointed, and feature marble-topped vanities and great views of either the Strip or the mountains.

Harrah's doesn't have much of a theme (none, actually), but its' location is perfect – flanking the Venetian and the Flamingo, and literally across from the Mirage and Caesar's Palace. A handy shopping arcade, a spacious but somewhat plain casino and a nice buffet are just some of the amenities that Harrah's offers.

Out back, this resort also features an Olympic-sized swimming pool with trellised gardens, a whirlpool, and a waterfall. A nearby health club and spa are also spacious and helpful additions to Harrah's.

Harrah's also features the funny, talented magician that plays each afternoon, Mac King, and a huge pool. Free shuttle service is just out back of the hotel, offering buses to the Rio, Main Street Station and Sam's Town. There is also a monorail station located here, making Harrah's a very convenient, stress-free place to stay and play.

Stratosphere

www.stratosphere.com. 1.702.380.7777. 2000 Las Vegas Blvd. South. 2,444 units. $49 and up. Daily resort fee: $24.99.

The Stratosphere, standing at 1,149 feet, is the tallest building west of the Mississippi, and a very striking hotel. A good mid-level resort with a bad location - poor Stratosphere. This resort is very self-contained, and for good reason – it is located at the very end of the Northern Strip, very close, actually, to downtown Vegas, which can be a good thing if you enjoy the vibrant downtown area of Las Vegas.

Rooms are pretty standard and feel like a nice three-star hotel, which the Stratosphere, in fact, is! Upgraded "Select" rooms are about ten dollars more a night, but we recommend them for their modern décor and more spaciousness.

The Stratosphere is home to several great restaurants, such as the Italian Fellini's, with amazing food, and also an affordable buffet and a nice food court. What sets this resort apart is not only its' observation tower and its' thrill rides, but the great prices it offers guests on a regular basis.

Take the elevator to the observation tower for some spectacular views of Vegas, and then ride the four thrill rides if you dare (see chapter 6). There are also some nice lounges, bars, and restaurants up here, and admission to the tower is included in your daily resort fee.

Treasure Island

www.treasureisland.com. **1.702.894.7111. 3300 Las Vegas Blvd. South. 2,885 units. $69 and up. Daily resort fee: $39.68.**

Right next to the tropical Mirage and connected by a short, fun tram ride, Treasure Island is a hotel with a muted pirate theme. This hotel used to be very family-friendly, and it is still somewhat, but much of the theming is gone. The TI, as it is known around town, still does boast some kid-friendly touches, such as a lush pool area, a Krispy Kreme, and the fun monorail ride to the Mirage, as we mentioned.

The exterior of the hotel, which is a light orange color, is striking, and the rooms are also very classy. Modern and full of marble touches, they are feature large soaking tubs in the bathroom and refrigerators. These rooms feel very deluxe, but are pretty affordable, as you can snag a room at many times of the year for as little as $69.

Senor Frogs, a nice 24-hour café, and a pricey but ample buffet are some of the dining options in Treasure Island. Several shops are handy, and the location of this resort is amazing - almost directly across from the Venetian, and next door to the Mirage. The TI is also a quick walk from the Fashion Show Mall, the Wynn and the Encore, as well as Trump Las Vegas. Yes, it's at the northern end of the Strip, but the location is fabulous.

Trump Las Vegas

www.trumphotels.com/las-vegas. 1.702.982.0000. 2000 Fashion Show Mall Drive, Las Vegas. Resort fee: $32.50.

Yes, this is THE hotel owned by the Trump organization, and it is a stunning resort. If you are at all familiar with other Trump properties worldwide, this is also a sumptuous 5-star winner, replete with all the bells and whistles.

Each room is a suite, and is at least 500 square feet. Floor-to-ceiling windows showcase the stunning views of either the mountains or the Las Vegas Strip. A huge European marble bathroom, and luxurious bedding abound, making you feel like a queen or a king here. Even the lobby bathrooms are enamored with gold (no, we were not surprised by this).

 Trump Las Vegas is also a condo complex, and many people actually live here part or full-time. You will still feel like a guest, however, because of the five-star, gracious service and myriad of amenities and location. Also, the location - right behind the Fashion Show Mall, and a short walk away from the Tropicana and the Wynn, is a winner in our opinion.

On our last visit to Vegas, we visited this resort, and jumped on the elevator, which whisked us up to the 64th floor, where we were greeted very warmly by two saleswomen. They informed us that we were free to look around a sample unit, and the sight from the windows was simply amazing.

A nice lobby bar, a gift shop, and a very swank restaurant are all found in the lobby. The seventh-floor pool and spa is very fancy and a nice way to spend a few stress-free hours.

Center Strip featured hotel: The Venetian/Palazzo

www.venetian.com. 1.702.414.1000. 3355 Las Vegas Blvd. South. 7,093 units. $169 and up. Daily resort fee: $39.

The Venetian is truly a show-stopper. It is a very common sight to see tourists stop and simply gawk at how beautiful this hotel is. Hotel owner Sheldon Anderson meticulously recreated the famous city, from the inside and outside canals where gondoliers take you for a real gondola ride, to a stunning recreation of St. Mark's square built into a high-end shopping mall.

The Venetian is, in one word - amazing. Truly a world-famous hotel, visitors flock from every country to stay and play here. It is a fabulous recreation of the famous Italian city, and the romance and colors of Venice come alive here. From the outside canals that continue to the Grand Canal Shoppes, the gondoliers that truly will sing to you, and then on to the stunning interior, the Venetian is a major bang for your buck.

The Palazzo is the sister hotel of the Venetian, and has its own lobby and casino, but the rooms are very similar. This is a more sedate hotel, for sure, but you are a short walk from the Venetian. As expected, the Palazzo is quieter, as we mentioned, and not as glitzy, but it is also a definite five-star hotel, with all the bells and whistles that the Venetian offers.

The casinos as both properties are both very ornate and feel upscale. The Venetian's sprawling casino emits a very unique smell – vanilla, maybe? Whatever it is, we like it, as we also like the wide variety of both slot and table games that these casinos offer.

Serenity now!

Many Las Vegas resorts boast spas, and the Venetian's Canyon Ranch spa is one of the best in town! Treatments include facials, massages, and there is even a full-service hair salon. Prices are high, but the quality is excellent. and the staff is gracious.

Each suite in both hotels is enormous – actually the size of a small apartment, at around 700 square feet, and boasts a sunken living area, minibar, seating area, and fabulous views of either the Strip or the mountains. Three flat-screen tvs are an added bonus. Whatever room you manage to snag, your room will have an amazing view.

The pool areas in both resorts are a bit ho-hum, although pleasant, but still try to spend at least a few hours lounging here and soaking up some rays.

The Venetian features over 20 restaurants and cafes, many of which are in the Grand Canal Shoppes. We can vouch for many of these, including the delicious Canaletto, which overlooks the flawless recreation of St. Mark's Square. A very good food court, featuring Italian and American options, can be found on the casino level.

Prices: Tend to be in the high 100's or low 200's, which is a steal for a 5-star hotel like the Venetian. We have heard reports that this hotel is on priceline, so be sure to try it in the North Strip section (5-star) of the name-your-own-hotel option.

Live la dolca vita at the Venetian and the Palazzo!

Hot tip!

Be sure to eat on the canal at the Grand Canal Shoppes. Take a break from the fun shops and pick one of the nice restaurants that overlook the canals inside this swank shopping mall. You will feel like you are really in Venice as you nosh on what will what surely will be a tasty meal, and watch real gondoliers paddle by with happy customers. The experience is truly one-of-a-kind in Vegas!

Wynn & Encore

www.wynnlv.com. 1.702.770.7100. 3131 Las Vegas Blvd. South. 4,750 units. $159 and up. Daily resort fee: $35

From casino genius Steve Wynn, the Wynn is his namesake hotel, and a beautiful one at that. It lacks the theming of the Bellagio, but still evokes a Bellagio-style feel, and is a sheer pleasure to visit. The rooms are large, and all suites, at over 700 square feet, much like the other hotels listed here. Windows are floor-to-ceiling, and feature gorgeous views of either the Las Vegas strip or the mountains.

The pool area is lush, and is a main reason to stay here, with stunning views and pampered service. It makes a hot, sweltering day in Vegas seem bearable, and relaxing. Wynn also boasts a wide selection of restaurants and cafes, including SW Steakhouse, and of course, great shopping and entertainment options.

The Encore is a sister property, and looks and feels very similar to the Wynn. Rooms here are also suites and will pamper you with amazing views, not to mention the marble-clad bathrooms and upscale furnishings.

Downtown area

Vegas regulars will tell you that downtown and the Strip are only a few miles apart, but vastly different. The Strip is more upscale and downtown feels a bit grungier and not as clean or upscale. Still, however, this area has grown much nicer in the last ten years, and now features several venerable hotels and attractions that should delight most visitors.

Even if you are a die-hard fan of the Las Vegas Strip, make sure to at least give this area a few hours of your time. The downtown area is located about a mile north of the Stratosphere.

Fun fact!

Many downtown hotels do not have a resort fee, which can mean a huge savings if you are staying for more than a few nights. Keep this fact in mind when budgeting for your Las Vegas vacation.

When we stayed at Main Street Station a few years ago, we used their free, and very convenient, shuttle bus that runs continuously to and from Harrah's, located mid-Strip. The service is very easy, and open to all guests who visit Las Vegas.

Advantages to staying downtown

It is also much easier to jump from hotel to hotel, as they are so close to each other. Keep in mind , however, that the notorious theming of hotels that you will see on the Strip is not here the in downtown hotels. The theming, when it is present, is much more muted. These are locals hotels – they appeal much more to the locals than the big, gaudy Strip hotels. Some hate this, and some love it – just keep it in mind when booking.

The Fremont Street experience, which is basically a free light show each night on an overhead canopy that covers some of this street, is also a plus. Guests can walk right out of their room to see the cacophony of lights, sounds, and party-goers revelling and drinking.

Another plus to staying at a downtown hotel? ***The prices are almost always cheaper here!*** Yes, you can snag a room for around $20 a night, and the value is high. Why are the prices so much cheaper here? Well, the hotels are more a hotel and not a resort, so there are not as many amenities that you need to pay for, like a spa or a pool. Also, the demand is simply not as high here as it is for Strip hotels, because these are where most visitors want to stay, so the prices are lower – simple supply and demand.

Map of Fremont Street (downtown area)

_____ = Fremont Street

Main Street Station / California (Main Street)

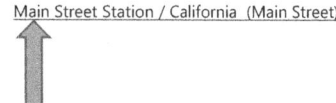

| * **Plaza** | *Las Vegas Club | *Binion's | *Fremont | | * El Cortez |

Featured Hotel – Downtown – Main Street Station

www.mainstreetstation.com. 1.702.387.1896. 200 North Main Street. 406 units. $49 and up. No resort fee.

The venerable Main Street Station is still a favorite among many Vegas regulars, especially those visiting from Hawaii – (go figure!). Its' sister hotel, the California, is connected to Main Street Station by an interior bridge, and leads you directly to the casino and restaurants of the California. Both hotels are similar, but we prefer Main Street Station. It evokes the history and feel of 19th century San Francisco, and the smallish, almost intimate feel of the casino is a nice change of pace from many of the larger, gaudier Las Vegas hotels. Stained glass windows and ornate chandeliers really hammer home this theme in a nice, subtle manner.

There is not a pool here, but guests receive free access to the small pool at its' sister hotel California, which is connected by an interior tunnel. The pool is tiny, but a helpful amenity nonetheless. Most hotels downtown do not have a pool, so this is a plus.

The Triple 7 Brew Pub, which your authors frequented during their last trip to Vegas, is a classic sports bar that offers tasty food. It is very convenient, and open until 2 am most nights. The Garden Court Buffet is one of the best in town, and offers amazingly affordable prices. A lunch is your best bet here, at around $8 for adults, and dinner is just a bit more, at around $10 for adults. The selections are wide, and the space is pretty, with lots of flowers and nice little touches.

After dinner, head outside and take a quick stroll to the heart of the downtown area, with the Fremont Street attraction just a few blocks away from Main Street Station.

Fun Fact!

There is an actual piece of the Berlin Wall in the men's restroom adjacent to the lobby. Check it out, men!

Other Recommended Downtown hotels

California

www.thecal.com. 1.702.385.1222. 12 Ogden Ave. 781 units. $40 and up. No resort fee.

Connected to Main Street Station by an interior tunnel, this is a very intimate hotel with a smaller casino and some great dining options. Is the theme California? Truthfully, we can't spot a theme, but this hotel, along with Main Street Station, is nearly always occupied, eighty percent, in fact, by Hawaiians, who love Vegas. Who knew, right?

The California is a very easy, breezy hotel, much like the real California. A two-minute walk from Fremont Street, it is ideally situated in the downtown area. Rooms are nicely appointed – not too fancy, but functional, with modern, light furniture and spacious bathrooms.

The California boasts a small pool that can get very crowded - try to hit it very early or late in the day. A small casino is well-stocked with all the slot machines and table games you can desire, and the California and Main Street Station share several souvenir shops and small eateries.

As you board the escalator to leave the California to head to Main Street Station, you will find a very handy donut/ ice cream shop in the upstairs connector. This place has low prices on donuts and coffee that will make starting your day very easy!

Four Queens

www.fourqueens.com. 1.702.385.4011. 202 Fremont Street. 690 units. $39 and up. No resort fee.

Named after the original owner's four daughters (ahhh, so sweet), this smaller hotel opened in 1966 with only 12 rooms, and is located smack dab on Fremont Street. It boasts a nice food court, a coffee shop, and Hugo's Cellar, a venerable, pricey restaurant. The feel of Four Queens is old-fashioned and ornate, with lots of gold touches everywhere. Right outside is a very handy Tix 4 Tonight ticket booth, one of several in Vegas, that give discounts on nearly all shows and attractions in Vegas.

The casino is airy and boasts a beautiful, huge glass chandelier that soars over the gaming area. Small but cozy, the casino, like the entire Four Queens itself, may appeal most to guests who don't want or care about a huge, glitzy Vegasy hotel experience.

There is no pool at the Four Queens, which can be a bummer to some guests, so plan accordingly if you are a big pool person! If you want to spend about the same as staying at Four Queens, you may want to book either the California or Main Street Station, as they both have access to a small pool.

Golden Gate Hotel and Casino

www.goldengatecasino.com. 1.702.385.1906. 1 Fremont Street. 122 units. $25 and up. No resort fee.

This hotel was the very first in the entire state of Nevada, opening in 1906 as the Nevada Hotel. Antique slot machines still abound, but touches of modernity, such as go-go dancers and modern rooms make the Golden Gate a nice blend of new and old.

The Golden Gate Hotel and Casino is ideally located in the heart of the Fremont Street experience. This small, boutique hotel is perfect for visitors who don't need a large, brash Vegas hotel experience. Located less than half a mile from at least three other hotels in the downtown cluster, the Golden Gate is a very convenient hotel to stay, as you can simply exit this hotel and pop in and out of neighboring hotels very easily.

The theme here is, as the name suggests, 1930's San Francisco, and subtle touches are everywhere. Rooms are small, but boast flatscreen tvs and iPod radios, and are done up in pleasant shades of red and brown.

Note that there is no pool here, but the location and amenities are great. Two restaurants are at the Golden Gate, including a deli that serves their famous shrimp cocktail, which is only around two dollars, and it is delicious! The budget-minded guests will get a lot for their money here.

Golden Nugget

www.goldennugget.com. 1.702.385.7111. 129 East Fremont Street. 2,425 units. $69 and up. Daily resort fee: $31.08.

This is, without a doubt, one of the real jewels of not just the downtown hotel scene, but in all of Vegas. It is very reminiscent of a Strip hotel, and was built by Steve Wynn in 1946. Very swank, but not pretentious, The Golden Nugget evokes the feel of the Bellagio, but being a downtown hotel gives visitors the advantage of having Fremont Street outside your door, and also being able to take a side trip to the Strip for a day of fun is a plus.

The pool complex here is amazing, as you can swim in a downright gorgeous pool complex replete with a sandy beach. The pool also features a very cool waterslide that runs through a glass tunnel in a shark tank - yes, there are actual sharks here.

The Golden Nugget also boasts a very nice spa, tennis courts, and a casino shuttle that ferries guests to and from the downtown casinos. Rooms in the newer Rush Tower are about $25 more a night, but it may be worth it for the minibars and leather furnishings here.

The buffet is a bit pricier than those at other downtown hotels, but is still a steal compared to buffets of other similarly-priced hotels on the Strip. After a tasty meal here, wander outside and explore the fun of the downtown area, with a myriad of souvenir shops and over a dozen hotels clustered right next to each other, just waiting to be explored.

Plaza Hotel

www.plazahotel.com. 1.844.698.2575. 1 Main Street, Las Vegas. 1,037 units. $59 and up. No resort fee.

This place used to be a bit on the grungy side, and was nothing to truly boast about. A few years, ago, however, the Plaza received a nice facelift, and is now a nice upscale resort. The look and feel is very four-star, and it is ideally situated in the heart of the Fremont Experience. A one-minute walk from both the California and Main Street Station, staying at the Plaza therefore offers guests many dining and entertainment options.

Rooms at the Plaza have been ungraded in recent years, and are decked out with marble-topped vanities and 32-inch flatscreen tvs. Some rooms overlook the pool complex, and are 400 - square - feet. These rooms feature expansive patios, which is a unique experience in downtown Las Vegas, where very few hotels even have a pool complex. This one is very nice too, with ample shade and cabanas for rent.

A small food court with a Krispy Kreme and a McDonalds is front and center in the lobby, as well as a popular breakfast place, Hash House A Go Go. Oscar's Steakhouse, owned by the former mayor, Oscar B. Goodman, is a popular watering hole and restaurant with mouth-watering steaks and other American fare.

The Plaza has an expansive casino, decked out in modern décor, and it boasts a huge bingo parlor. This resort packs quite a punch, and, much like other downtown resorts, rates here are very reasonable, starting at around $59 and up a night.

East of the Strip

The hotels east of the Strip are very nice, but tend to not be as themed as other areas in Vegas. Many are within easy walking distance of the Strip, and this area is generally safe and appealing. UNLV, the University of Nevada, Las Vegas, is located here, as is McCarran International Airport.

Featured Hotel-East of the Strip: Hard Rock Hotel

www.hardrocklasvegas.com. 1.702.693.5000. 4455 Paradise Rd (at Harmon Ave.) Las Vegas. 1,500 units. $89 and up. Resort fee: $14.99.

Music lovers, check this hotel out. The hip, savvy Hard Rock Hotel is overlooked by many guests, and clearly caters to the younger set. Within walking distance to the Strip, the Hard Rock Hotel and Casino is a very unique place that certainly won't appeal to everyone. As you enter this hotel, you will see very quickly that the median age and body fat percentage of the guests has all dropped, and the cool factor is everywhere.

Rooms are sleek and modern, with nice amenities like contemporary bathrooms and a black-and-gray design scheme in the newest Paradise Tower. The pool area features a sandy beach and a lazy river, and plenty of young, hot people!

You can nosh at fun eateries like Pink Taco and Culinary Dropout, which is casual and perfect for the clientele of this hotel. There is no buffet, here, however, but the Strip and all its' buffets are a short walk away.

The Hard Rock is really known for its' party vibe. The Rehab dance club is legendary, and the pool area is always teeming with young guys and gals ready to party. Families will not be as happy here, but this place teems with happy singles, especially during spring break and summer time. Rates are reasonable.

Other Recommended Hotels

Marriott's Grand Chateau

www.marriott.com. 1.702.862.5600. 75 East Harmon Ave. Las Vegas. 643 units. $120 and up. No resort fee.

If you are familiar with any Marriott worldwide, this hotel won't shock you, and will look very familiar. We are big fans of the Marriott chain, as they all seem to be pretty consistent and polished, and the Grand Chateau is no different. If you're wondering, "Grand Chateau" means "big castle" in French, and no, this is not castle-themed, but it is a pretty big hotel. The hotel is situated right off the Strip, and very close to the Miracle Mile shopping center, which is in Planet Hollywood.

Rooms are all spacious, and you can book either a studio or a one or two-bedroom suite. Studios feature microwaves, a mini-fridge, and a small kitchen. One and two-bedroom suites feature even more amenities, and the two-bedroom suites even feature washer and dryers, which is very handy. A nice rooftop pool, a gym, and several dining options round out the amenities. There is no casino here, but there are many within walking distance.

The Marriott Grand Chateau features a lobby bar, The Marketplace, which offers snacks and Starbucks coffee, Sky Bar 38, a trendy rooftop bar, and also Level 5 Pool Bar and Grill. If you are seeking a very sedate, calm hotel with no casino but lots of amenities, this may be the place for you.

Platinum

www.platinumlasvegas.com. 1.702.365.5000. 211 East Flamingo Rd, Las Vegas. Resort fee: $25.60.

An all-suite hotel, Platinum is a unique place to call home for your stay in Vegas. In addition to a very swank hotel, the Platinum is also a condo complex, and many owners rent out their suites. It is one of those places that not every visitor knows about, but when you stay here, you often don't want to stay anywhere else!

The Platinum feels very much feels like a resort, which it is – a small one, anyway. There is no casino here, but the hotel/condo does boast an indoor and an outdoor pool, plus a restaurant that serves both breakfast and lunch. The resort also boasts a sundries shop, room service from 6 am until 11 pm, and a full-service concierge and fitness and business centers.

Views here are amazing from the outdoor observatory, overlooking the Strip, which is an especially special spot at night, when the whole city is light up like a giant Christmas tree.

A pleasant restaurant featuring American cuisine, as well as a lobby bar are located downstairs, and the pool has amazing views of the Strip, which is only a few safe-to-walk blocks away.

Suites are huge, surpassing even some rooms at the Wynn and the Venetian – all for a lot less a night! The suites start at a whopping 950 feet, and offer both one and two-bedroom units, with luxurious amenities such as marble-topped vanities and plush bedding. The views of either the Las Vegas strip or the mountains are gorgeous.

West of the Strip

Several top hotels are located west of the Strip, although you will need a good shuttle, for the most part, to reach the Strip. The good news? Almost all hotels in this region feature free hotel shuttles that transport you directly to and from the Strip.

Palace Station

www.palacestation.com. 1.702. 367.2411. 2411 West Sahara Ave. 1,001 units. $29 and up. Daily resort fee: $17.

For those seeking a low-key value right near the Strip, look no further! Palace Station is one of our favorite hotels, and it located very close to the Strip, about a mile from Circus Circus. A very handy, free shuttle connects guests from Palace Station to both the airport and the Strip.

Palace Station offers a handful of restaurants including a great buffet and café, a spacious casino and a bingo parlor. Rooms are nice but a bit bland, but for prices that start at $29, who's complaining? The cheapest rooms can be found in the two-story courtyard buildings, and are functional but nice. This is a great option for a very affordable trip to Vegas.

West of the Strip: Recommended Hotel – Rio All-Suite Hotel and Casino

www.riolv.com. 1.702.777.7777. 3700 West Flamingo Rd, Las Vegas. 2,582 units. $99 and up. Daily resort fee: $30.

The Rio is infamous in Vegas for its younger clientele and party atmosphere. Inspired by the beautiful Rio de Janeiro, the Rio Las Vegas is dramatic in appearance (see photo), with its stark red and blue appearance. Oddly, the interior is not too special, and doesn't exactly evoke Rio, which we still think is a bit strange, but It does boast an award-winning buffet, a shopping arcade, a sprawling casino, and a host of restaurants. Famed illusionists Penn & Teller perform here. For some reason, young people seem to love this duo, with their off-color humor and bevy of funny illusions.

Very easy to get to, the Rio is accessible by a free shuttle that runs to and from Harrah's, which is conveniently located mid-Strip. Every room is actually a suite, which seems to be the new thing in Vegas. Over 700 square feet, almost all feature floor-to-ceiling windows with killer views of the mountains or the Las Vegas Strip.

The famous VooDoo lounge is found on the roof, and serves as an indoor/outdoor nightclub and restaurant. Reviews of this lounge are generally very positive, and (surprise, surprise), the VooDoo attracts scores of younger guests each night.

The Rio is certainly worth at least a few nights, even if you are travelling as a family or an older couple. Yes, the clientele is younger here than most other casinos, but the fun atmosphere and myriad of facilities here make it worth a stay.

Other Recommended West Strip hotels – The Gold Coast

www.goldcoastcasino.com. 1.702.367.7111. 4000 West Flamingo Rd, Las Vegas. 711 units. $39 and up. Daily resort fee: $17.99.

This smaller hotel and casino is right next to the Palms and across from the Rio. It is not the most exciting hotel, but still claims some nice amenities, especially for a family, like a handy 70-lane bowling alley, a solid food court and buffet, and a small but clean pool.

Rooms are nicely updated, with marble touches, and nice views of the mountains or nearby Strip. The hotel itself is not themed, but is a smaller and cozier, much like a downtown hotel.

As mentioned, the Gold Coast Ports of Call buffet is a great value with tasty, fresh food. Gold Coast also has a TGI Friday's and the award-winning Ping Pang Pong Chinese restaurant. The casino is small and bright, and a free shuttle ferries guests from the Gold Coast to the Strip and its' sister property, The Orleans.

The Orleans

www.orleanscasino.com. 1.702.365.7111. 4500 West Tropicana Ave, Las Vegas. 1,866 units. $49 and up. Daily resort fee: $17.99.

Mardi Gras, anyone? Despite being relatively isolated, the Orleans is a very nice, picturesque hotel that brings its guests the flavor of New Orleans. Larger than its' sister property, The Gold Coast, The Mardi Gras theme extends to the casino and colorful exterior of the hotel.

A nice buffet, food court, a nicely landscaped pool area, and a handful of shops are just some of the helpful amenities that The Orleans offers its' guests. Kids and adults alike will enjoy the 70-lane bowling alley and the 18-screen movie theater. This is truly a self-contained resort.

This charming hotel extends the New Orleans theme throughout the casino and lobby, resulting in a very colorful recreation of the distinctive New Orleans-style architecture. A complimentary shuttle runs from the Orleans to the Gold Coast, and also to the Strip.

Palms

www.palms.com. 1.702.942.7777. 4321 West Flamingo Rd, Las Vegas. 1,302 units. $99 and up. Daily resort fee: $36.27.

Very similar in clientele to the Hard Rock and the Rio, the Palms is party central. To be honest, the theming here is nonexistent, but the Palms does have a lot to offer. The location is off the Strip, right next to the Gold Coast, and a short walk to the Rio, as well. A free shuttle conveniently connects the Palms to the Forum Shops at Caesars Palace, and runs throughout the day.

Rooms, in several towers, are contemporary in décor, and the Ivory Tower rooms are decked out with murals and colored in fuschia and silver and gray. Bathrooms here are modern and decked out in lots of marble. Most rooms are actually suites, and include kitchens with microwaves and stoves, so you get a lot for your money with the Palms.

The Palms offers a nice child-care facility, a great food-court, and also several happening nightspots, Moon and Ghostbar. The French restaurant, Alize, is highly recommended, and adds a touch of class to this very young, party-hardy resort.

The Palms pool complex, not surprisingly, is a hot party spot, day and night!

Hotels situated way off the Strip

The following four hotels are each located at least 20 minutes from the Strip, but each comes with a handy, free shuttle that will safely shuttle you to and from the Strip. For those visitors who want a bit more solitude, and who want to explore life outside the Strip and downtown, these hotels will do the trick.

Off-Strip Recommended Hotel - Sam's Town

www.samstown.com. **1.702.456.7777. 5111 Boulder Hwy, Las Vegas. 646 units. $39 and up. Resort fee: $16.**

Fun and affordable – these are the two adjectives many visitors choose to use when describing Sam's Town. Located about five short miles from the Strip, this hotel, favored by locals, offers guests a truly self-contained resort with a slightly western feel to it. A few shops, a great buffet and food court, a nicely appointed casino, a great pool, and a bowling alley are the main things that Sam's Town offers.

You can easily spend a day or two here, just enjoying the resort's many amenities. Sam's Town is a nice break from the huge, sprawling resorts on the Strip. Intimate, but not too small, this is a great resort to simply enjoy for a few days. Frequent, free shuttles running from Harrah's deliver guests to Sam's Town. The trip is quick and easy, and actually a fun way to see parts of the city that you otherwise might not.

As detailed in our Fun and Free chapter, this hotel also features a free light show called the Sam's Town Sunset Stampede, which the kids will love.

Green Valley Ranch, Resort and Spa

www.greenvalleyranch.sclv.com. 1.702.617.7777. 2300 Paseo Verde Pkwy, Henderson. 490 units. $99 and up. Daily resort fee: $36.47

A true winner of a resort, Green Valley is a very self-contained place that caters to both kids and adults. The exterior is Mediterranean-inspired, with red-tiled roofs and towering palms. Inside, this four-star property features opulent, rooms with patios and marble-topped vanities, and many amenities, including a spa, salon, nice pool complex, and diverse dining options.

Located in Henderson, and a free, twenty-minute shuttle ride from the Strip, Green Valley Ranch features a very affordable and ample Feast Buffet, a pizza parlor, and also a Grand Café, among other dining options. The Backyard, their expansive pool complex, offers cabanas for rent, outdoor Jacuzzis, and a bridge that spans the glittering pools.

A casino featuring all the games is inside, and is also nicely decorated. Bingo is also offered here, which you don't find everywhere. Regal Cinemas, a giant movie complex, is onsite, and a huge arcade will also appeal to the kids in your party. Green Valley Ranch really has something for everyone, and the price, at about $99 and up a night, is also very appealing.

Hilton Lake Las Vegas – Henderson

www.hilton.com. 1.702.567.4700. 1610 Lake Las Vegas Parkway, Henderson, 89011. 349 units. $99 and up. Daily resort fee: $25.

A stunning and not all that well-known hotel, the Hilton Lake Las Vegas a true gem. Situated directly on the shores of beautiful Lake Las Vegas and directly adjacent to the marina of this lake, with all the shops and restaurants, this Hilton packs quite a punch.

The Hilton is located in suburban Henderson, a nice town with several locals hotels. This hotel is about a twenty-minute drive from the Strip. If you're worried about being too far out, don't worry, as there is a complimentary 4pm shuttle each day, as well as taxis and shuttle services you can hire.

For around $100 a night, you will get a lot for your money. Nicely appointed rooms, with lots of marble, a pool that overlooks a perfect recreation of the famous Ponte Vecchio bridge on the lake, and a nice spa are just a few of the amenities you will enjoy as a guest here.

For those not familiar with Lake Las Vegas, this is a beautiful place to spend a few stress-free hours, shopping and dining. The architecture, shops, and restaurants are all Italian-inspired, and, simply put, if you love Italy, like we do, you will probably enjoy staying here.

Recommend hotel - Red Rock Canyon Resort and Spa

www.redrock.sclv.com. 1.702.797.7777.11011 West Charleston Blvd, Las Vegas. 816 units. $150 and up. Daily resort fee: $36.15.

This beautiful resort, created by the makers of the also amazing Green Valley Ranch, is located about 20 miles from the Strip, and offers scenic views of the mountains. It boasts luxurious rooms filled with lots of marble amenities.

A stunning exterior leads you into a sumptuous hotel that offers a spa and salon, a nice casino, a bingo parlor, and even a movie theater. The pool area is very nice, and offers gorgeous views of the nearby Red Rock Canyon and the mountains.

Rooms are very luxurious, and are adorned with 42-inch plasma HD tvs and fully-stocked private bars. Marble-topped bathrooms will pamper you with 15-inch LCD tvs and deep soaking tubs. The feel is upscale, simply put, and we recommend this hotel if you want a taste of luxury away from the bustling Strip.

Guests also enjoy the nearby, very popular Red Rock Canyon natural habitat, adjacent to the hotel.

Chapter 4 – Fun and Free Las Vegas

Free? In Las Vegas? Yes, there are many options for a free attraction here, and many are over-looked by many visitors to this amazing city. Many guests assume that all attractions are pricey, but many are absolutely free, and can make your trip a bit less expensive. We want you to be aware of all the cool, free stuff that Sin City has to offer. Here are our top picks…

Bellagio: Conservatory, Gardens & Fountains

www.bellagio.com. 1.702.693.7111. 3600 Las Vegas Blvd. South.

Yes, Bellagio is a world-famous destination, and many visitors know about their dancing fountains. Walking up to this Italian delight of a hotel is a sight, as the exterior is a stunning masterpiece of architecture. Many guests simply stop and gawk, then grab their camera for some pictures of this stunning resort.

Conservatory & Gardens

Hours: 24/7

Directly inside the front doors, and just next to the check-in desk lies the Bellagio Conservatory and Gardens, which is not to be missed. This always present garden is moderate in size, and always themed. Being that this is the ornate Bellagio, this is an over-the-top affair, with themes such as the holidays or the beach. Rows and rows of brilliant flowers help enhance the theme of the conservatory. Bring your camera!

Fountains & Water Ballet

Hours: 3pm to midnight. Every half-hour from 3pm until 7pm, and then every half-hour until midnight.

Directly in front of the Bellagio is a huge lake where a synchronized fountain show of water jets erupts every afternoon, sending water 250 feet in the air! Each musical piece is timed perfectly to the accompanying bursts of water and lights.

The fountains are a huge crowd pleaser, and very enchanting – you have to see this one to really believe it. Even after our many visits to Las Vegas, we are still mesmerized by the

Bellagio's water ballet. The show, with accompanying music, is also very relaxing, which, in Vegas, can be a great thing, as the rest of the city seems to hum with almost nervous excitement.

Hot Tip!

The best view of this water ballet can be had across the street at the Eiffel Tower attraction, or at a restaurant at either Paris or Planet Hollywood, where you can eat & ogle the fountains. Mon Ami Gabi, a quaint sidewalk café at Paris, is a prime spot for enjoying the show. The show starts at 3 pm, 7 days a week, and runs every half-hour from 3pm to 7pm, and every 15 minutes, from 7 pm to midnight.

Circus Circus : The Circus

www.circuscircus.com. 2880 Las Vegas Blvd. South. 1.702. 734.0410. Hours: 24/7

Yes, this is a real circus! The world's largest permanent circus is located at this kid-friendly hotel on the North side of the Strip. Kid-friendly is an understatement here, as yours will most likely love this attraction.

There are the typical games that you must pay for – but you could win a prize, which will make the kids smile! The actual circus, however, is always free.

Jugglers and trapeze artists, many of whom come from all over the world, are just some of the entertainment that your kids, or grandkids, will love. After watching these talented performers, do make time for a few rides at the Adventuredome, also at Circus Circus (see chapter 8). Alas, sadly, these are not free!

Make sure to also check out the fun shops right outside the Adventuredome park, and also simply explore this kitschy, kid-friendly resort. Your kids will thank you, trust us!

Flamingo Habitat

www.caesars.com. 1.702.733.3111. 3555 Las Vegas Blvd. South. Hours: From dawn to dusk. Feedings at 8 am and 2:30 pm.

This is a jewel that many visitors simply overlook, usually because they don't know about it. We were enchanted by our visit here on our last trip, and spent at least a half-hour just wandering around and appreciating this outdoor exhibit.

The Flamingo hotel is situated ideally center strip, and directly behind the hotel is this habitat teaming with flamingoes, exotic fish, turtles, and swans. Handy informational plaques educate visitors about each animal here. You can wander the shops at the Flamingo, a Vegas old-timer hotel, then casually exit the building and bump, literally, into this exhibit, as we did!

Las Vegas is almost always sunny and pleasant, of course, so this makes for a great attraction almost any month of the year, as it is completely outside. Rarely is the habitat too busy, and it is a smaller attraction, so feel free to try it anytime.

Fremont Street Experience

www.vegasexperience.com. **Hours: 24/7**

The sometimes seedy downtown area has gotten much cleaner and more upscale in the last ten years, and is now a very amusing and safe place to spend a few hours. The Fremont Street Experience is highlighted by a giant canopy over the length of Fremont Street, which is a central street surrounding many downtown hotels.

Each night, the mammoth canopy lights up with glowing, flashing lights, creating quite a spectacular scene. Visitors can also pay a hefty fee to zipline down the entire length of this canopy, and it is a sight to see this as you meander down Fremont Street.

After experiencing this free spectacle, there are a few hotels to explore. The Golden Nugget, Four Queens, and Main Street Station are all within a three-minute walk away, and are worth exploring. Each is a unique hotel, and deserves some extra time and attention. Be sure to experience some of the other hotels, as well, including Golden Gate and the Plaza, and to explore their respective casinos, as well.

Parents, take notice, however – at night, like in some Strip hotels, you will see scantily clad go-go girls in some hotels here in the downtown hotels. The atmosphere here is definitely more adult-oriented, but you will see many, many kids, of course, wherever you go in Vegas.

The Las Vegas Strip

www.vegas.com. www.tripadvisor.com. Hours: 24/7.

Yes, dear readers, this is a free attraction, and in our minds, one of the best free attractions in the world! The Strip is to Vegas what Times Square is to New York. The action, the people watching, the beautiful, almost unbelievably massive, themed resorts that tower over the Strip...all of it is pretty amazing! You must spend at least a day or so roaming the Strip, and popping in and out of the casinos. Not all hotels, of course, are themed, but to us, these are the

most fun ones to explore. After spending even twenty minutes in a hotel like Bellagio, you may well feel like you have just stepped into paradise.

Our recommendation? Start at one end of the Strip and just start exploring. We personally like to start at Mandalay Bay and then continue up the Strip until we reach Circus Circus, a trek that takes about two hours or so, if you pop into some hotels on the way, of course. We also enjoy stopping at the Bellagio and then making our way into the Forum Shops next door for a bit of shopping and a snack.

If walking is too much, there are many monorails and Deuce buses, not to mention taxis, that can help you cover the whole Strip. (covered in chapter one).

Certainly stop for a nice, leisurely buffet or café lunch, and rest your feet. You can even treat yourself to a few rides at the Adventuredome at Circus Circus, at the end of our recommended journey down the Strip. You've earned it!

Mirage's Volcano

www.mirage.com. 1.702.791.7111. 3400 Las Vegas Blvd. South. Hours: Sundays-Thursdays, 8 and 9 pm. Fridays and Saturdays 8, 9 and 10 pm.

Every night, an interesting thing happens at the very tropical, mid-Strip hotel, the Mirage. A faux volcano erupts, and, although, a bit cheesy, it is a fun sight, especially for kids. It has recently been ungraded, and now features even large fireballs and a pleasant coconut scent that permeates the area.

Scads of tourists line up about ten minutes or so before the volcano erupts, so get a good place and have fun! After the big event, head into the tropical oasis that is the Mirage and reward yourself with a fruity drink or two.

Inside the classy resort, the theming is immaculate, and transports you to a very nice, tropical place – Fiji, perhaps, with tons of foliage and a huge aquarium behind the front desk.

Sam's Town Sunset Stampede Laser Light Show

www.samstown.com. 1.702.456.7777. 5111 Boulder Hwy, Las Vegas. Hours: 2 pm, 4 pm, 6 pm, 8 pm, and 10 pm.

Sam's Town is a self-contained resort and casino, and located inside this charming and western-theme resort, this attraction is a fun and kitschy attraction for any visitor, especially kids. The show features moving, animatronic animals, lasers, dancing waterfalls, and even fake snow in the wintertime. We can't quite capture this show in one sentence, but let's just call it fun and very kid and adult-friendly.

Make sure to spend at least an hour doing another fun thing, which is also free – exploring this beautiful, relaxing resort! Sam's Town has a smaller, cozy casino, a great food court, a top-notch buffet, a small collection of restaurants, and a few shops. Easily accessed by a free shuttle from Harrah's, make sure to carve out some time here during your trip.

Welcome to Las Vegas Sign

www.vegas.com. www.tripadvisor.com. **Hours: 24/7**

The iconic Welcome to Las Vegas" is a fun and free attraction in itself. We actually saw it accidentally, on a tour bus, as we swung back to our hotel! It is a quick drive from most hotels on the Strip, as it is located on the Strip, about a mile south of Mandalay Bay, which is the southernmost hotel clustered right on the Strip.

The sign is quite an iconic landmark, and you will often spot tourists making a special pilgrimage here to see it for themselves.

Wynn Lake of Dreams

www.wynnlv.com. 1.702.770.7100. 3131 Las Vegas Blvd. South. Hours: Every half-hour, from dusk until 11:30 pm.

OK, so this is kind of free, and kind of not, so, let us explain. The Wynn has created a very

Cool light show complete with a 40-ft tall waterfall and a whopping 4,000 lights. The show also features a bevy of music and imagery, which all results in a very unique experience.

To actually see the show, however, you need to either enjoy a drink at a bar called Parasol Down, or have dinner at either SW Steakhouse or the Lakeside restaurant. Hence, this attraction is not exactly free, but it is a nice addition to either dining or drinking experience!

Chapter 5 – The Vegas Shopping Scene

New York, Milan and Vegas? Yes, it's actually up there, folks, although this point is highly subjective. For us, however, and for millions of visitors, Las Vegas is one of the top shopping destinations in the country, if not the world.

So you came to Las Vegas to shop? Well, you are certainly not the only one. Your humble authors love to shop! Yes, most visitors come to experience Vegas, but one could literally spend each day shopping and not be bored.

Simply put - Vegas has it all. From very high-end shops like Versace and Chanel, to the self-proclaimed world's largest souvenir shop, you will probably find exactly what you want in Las Vegas. There is a large variety of shops to suit anyone's taste.

Here are our favorites in the amazing Vegas shopping scene!

Best Overall Shopping Experience – The Forum Shops at Caesar's Palace.

Best Overall luxury shopping collection – Bellagio's shopping promenade.

Best Overall Outdoor shopping experience – Premium Outlets North.

Best Luxury Shop – Michael Kors at the Venetian. Kors, if you are not familiar with the popular designer, is known for his bevy of sleek and stylish purses, accessories and clothing that is expensive but not nearly as pricey as other luxury brands like Louis Vuitton.

Best local Vegas shop – The Bonanza Gift Shop, near Circus Circus. This is the largest self-proclaimed souvenir shop in the country! You can find just about anything here, from shot glasses to tee shirts. Check it out at : **www.bonanzagiftshop.com.**

Best Restaurant Pit Stop – The Cheesecake Factory at the Forum Shops at Caesar's is ideally located, and offers amazing, affordable food. The menu here is long!

Best sugar stop - Yes, we all need a boost of sugar from time to time, right? Well, you've come to the right place! Our favorite is the Ghirardelli shop at the outdoor Linq shopping pavilion (see below). Their milkshakes and chocolate squares will melt in your mouth, and will not break the bank.

<u>Most Underrated Shopping Experience</u> – The outdoor Linq Promenade between the Linq and Flamingo. There are funky clothing and accessory shops here, as well as a mouth-watering Ghirardelli chocolate shop. You must try their chocolate shakes – best in the world!

Atrium Shops at the Palazzo

<u>www.venetian.com. 1.702.414.1000. 3131 Las Vegas Blvd. South.</u>

Much like the Palazzo, itself, this smaller shopping plaza at the Palazzo is much like a mini, upscale department store. Located on the casino level, be prepared to bring your credit card or a lot of cash to chop here! Ritzy brands of liquor and cosmetics are sold, along with a multitude of fragrances.

Exquisite chandeliers, along with a colorful palette of umbrellas which hang from the ceilings make this a very happy place to shop. The feel here is very posh and upscale.

Perfumes and cosmetic brands like Chanel and Estee Lauder are here, along with very expensive liquor. Tom Ford, Burberry, Barney's New York and Salvatore Ferragamo are also featured retailers at the Atrium. You are also a very quick five-minute walk to the Grand Canal Shoppes at the Venetian, so, by all means, start here and keep on shopping!

Bellagio Shops

<u>www.bellagio.com. 1.702.693.7111. 3600 Las Vegas Blvd. South.</u>

The Bellagio is almost synonymous with luxury, and the collection of shops in the Bellagio is the epitome of luxe. Big names like Louis Vuitton, Fendi, Chanel, and Dior are all feature players, and this small shopping mall is airy and pleasant, and conveniently connected directly to the Bellagio casino. Just outside. Even if your bank account needs some help, you may well feel rich just walking down this shopping promenade.

Light and airy, the Bellagio Shops are tres upscale, and a number of upscale restaurants

like the revered Picasso, are located here, as well. The Shops also lead out to Caesar's Palace, which features the amazing Forum Shops.

Crystals

www.aria.com. 1.702.590.7757. 3730 Las Vegas Blvd. South.

Luxury abounds here, at Aria's Crystals shopping pavilion. Located conveniently on the monorail between Monte Carlo and Bellagio, Crystals is where you go to be seen and to shop till you drop! The feeling here is very modern, with crystal chandeliers and modern sculptures everywhere, so if that is not your thing, perhaps the shops will be to your liking!

Shops like Yves Saint Laurent and Tom Ford definitely cater to a certain upscale clientele, so be prepared to drop some cash if you want to shop here. This mall is fun to visit, much like the shopping promenade at Bellagio, and is in a prime location on the Strip, and for people watching.

Fashion Show Mall

www.thefashionshow.com. 1.702.369.8382. 3200 Las Vegas Blvd. South.

OK, so you came to Vegas to shop? Well, you may want to pencil the Fashion Show Mall into your itinerary. It is massive, and, yes, it does actually host runway shows, every week, usually on Tuesdays. These shows are fun to watch, and feel very Vegasy. The Fashion Show Mall boasts 25 restaurants, 8 departments stores, and 250 stores, so plan your time accordingly!

A large, well, um, spaceship sculpture sits on top of this mall (see photo), making it, visually, also a show-stopper. Noone quite knows what this is, but it's pretty cool! Stores include Nordstrom, Victoria's Secret, Coach, and the Disney Store. A variety of fast food outlets, like Wendy's are here, and full-service restaurants include Johnny Rockets, Ra Sushi, and Villa Italia Kitchen.

Right outside the Fashion Show Mall is Treasure Island on one side, and out back is Trump Las Vegas, which are both worth a visit. The Fashion Show Mall is also connected to the Wynn by a very convenient overhead bridge.

Forum Shops at Caesars Palace

www.forumshops.com. 1.702.731.7710. 3570 Las Vegas Blvd. South.

This high-end, beautiful mall is always among the most successful in America, based on annual sales. The ceiling here is a pretty blue with white cloud-like strokes, making the mall feel very light and airy. An addition to the existing mall, which was already massive, makes the place...well, even more massive, but a great place to shop for a few hours.

Our favorite shops here include Victoria's Secret, Juicy Couture, Lacoste, Guess, and H & M. There are also several Vegasy souvenir shops here, as well. The selection of restaurants and cafes, like the shop selection, is varied and there is truly something for everyone. The Cheesecake Factory, one of our favorites, is here, and is a surprisingly affordable option. Most restaurants here, however, like at the hotel at Caesar's itself, are inevitably pricey (We once ordered one scoop of gelato, and it cost us $14!), so be prepared!

Being Vegas, there is also a fun show featuring..., and, of course, kids and many adults love it. It is, in a word – Vegasy! This is a fun place to spend a few hours, and it is even more fun to gape at Caesar's beautiful, bright casino after your visit.

Grand Canal Shoppes at the Venetian

www.venetian.com. 1.702.414.1000. 3355 Las Vegas Blvd. South.

The Grand Canal Shoppes are a very amusing experience, even if shopping is not your thing, simply because they bring shoppers to a perfect recreation of Venice, and, more specifically, St.

Mark's Square in Venice. Like the Venetian hotel itself, the authenticity will blow you away the first time you see it. The colors and flavor transport you to Venice, making shopping here a real treat.

Just like the real Venice, there are many bridges to cross to get to the other side of this luxury emporium. Higher end stores include Michael Kors, bebe, Coach, and Jimmy Choo, and there is also a new Victoria's Secret store.

Quaint restaurants abound, many of which boast seats that overlook the canals. A new Cocolini Gelato just opened, and provides guests with amazing, creamy gelato, which is a healthier version of ice cream, and very popular in the real Italy!

A perfect recreation of St. Mark's Square is, of course, this mall's center piece, and, just as in the real city, there are a myriad of choice Italian restaurants, like our recommended Canaletto, covered in our dining chapter, which is smack dab in the center of the square. Pick a restaurant and definitely request a seat where you can do some prime people watching! There is also a nice food court with less expensive options.

After shopping for a few hours, head downstairs to the casino, which we regret to inform you, we never seem to win at, but we do still love. The casino and hotel, like the Grand Canal Shoppes, are elegant and upscale.

Top Pick - Linq Promenade

www.caesars.com/linq. 1.702.731.7710. 3570 Las Vegas Blvd. South.

The Linq Promenade is a relatively new, outdoor shopping plaza that is a refreshing addition to the Las Vegas shopping scene. Tucked between the new Linq hotel, which was formerly the Imperial Palace, and the Flamingo, this outdoor enclave is teeming with funky shops like Bella Scarpa, and eateries like the Honolulu Cookie Company, and the Ghirardelli Chocolate shop, with its' legendary shakes and chocolates.

The new High Roller, the world's tallest observation wheel, popular in other US and international cities, is here, also, at the rear of the Linq Promenade. This fun new attraction has become very popular in Vegas.

Miracle Mile Shops – Planet Hollywood

www.planethollywoodresort.com. **1.702.785.5555. 3667 Las Vegas Blvd. South.**

Yes, we still mourn the loss of the gorgeous Aladdin resort, which is now Planet Hollywood, but this shopping mall has at least retained its' Arabian theme. It is a delight to wander the atmospheric, winding halls of this mall, taking in the unique collection of shops and restaurants.

Over thirty dining options abound, like the great Mexican sit-down restaurant La Salsa Cantina, which serves great, authentic food. Here, you can sit and watch the always interesting flow of passing shoppers, which is always interesting. The popular Buffalo Wlld Wings, as well as Panda Express can be found at Miracle Mile. To quench your sweet tooth, check out Ben & Jerry's and Nestle Tollhouse Café.

Trendy shops like Sephora, Bikini Bay, Welcome to Las Vegas, and Houdini's Magic Shop make this shopping mall a nice place to spend a few hours.

Premium North Outlets

www.premiumnorthoutlets.com. 1.702.474.7500. 875 S. Grand Central Parkway, Las Vegas.

A real person can actually shop here, and not break the bank! National brands like Michael Kors, Neiman Marcus, Polo Ralph Lauren, Levi's, and Gap are all here, and most stores offer substantial savings - we're talking 25 to 65 % off of retail prices.

On a pleasant day (note: not summer!), the outlets are a great place to shop. You can positively roast on a hot summer day, however, as the stores are located outside, but there are plenty of cafes and restaurants like the Cheesecake Factory, as well as a nice food court to cool off in. Plus, ducking into an air-conditioned shop can really hit the spot.

Getting to the Premium Outlets is easy – simply take the Deuce double-decker city bus that stops at most hotels ($8 for an all-day pass) or a taxi. The outlets are located about 2 miles from the Stratosphere.

Top Pick – The Everything Coca-Cola Store

www.worldofcoca-cola.com. 1.702.270.5952. 3785 Las Vegas Blvd. South (at the Showcase Mall, in front of MGM Grand).

Can you get any more all-American than a Coca-Cola store?

Hands down, this is one of our favorite stores in the world! If you are even a moderate fan of Coke products, you must check out this store, which is really more of a homage to many people's favorite drink - Coke. Located inside the Showcase Mall, in front of MGM Grand, and across from Excalibur, the World of Coca-Cola is a two-level store and café solely featuring Coca-Cola products from around the world.

The first floor is a giant shopping emporium where you can find anything from a Coca-Cola tee-shirt to a Coca-Cola souvenir ball. The selection is varied and fun to sort through. Watch out for the crowds, though - this place gets busy fast!

Upstairs is divided almost equally into a store on one side and a small café serving Coca-Cola Coke floats and other treats. Our recommendation? Try the affordable sample tray of Coke products from around the world. It is only $9, and you get 16 Small samples of Coke from countries like Italy and Israel. We had to finish every drop – yes, it was that good! This store is just too much fun!

There is a handy Outback Restaurant and the M&M Shop is also right next door, making this a handy spot to shop for a few hours. Most visitors seem to really enjoy this atmospheric and all-American shop.

Chapter 6 – Dining in Las Vegas

Where do we even start on this topic?

Dining in Las Vegas is synonymous with variety and exciting new restaurants. The dining scene has boomed in the last ten years, and can please even the pickiest of eaters. Vegas is one of the top places in the world for foodies, with high-end restaurants, great desserts, and amazing, expansive buffets that will leave you wanting more.

Big name chefs like Joel Robuchon and Thomas Keller are here, with their posh restaurants that come with amazing service and, of course, big prices. If you're into this type of dining, you can't go wrong in Vegas. Lesser expensive options abound, of course, with many handy food courts and smaller cafes and restaurants. Big chains like the Cheesecake Factory are here, as well as local Vegas favorites.

Buffets, of course, are a dime a dozen, and almost all are a good quality. We will detail our top buffet picks later in the chapter. One of our favorite things in Vegas to do is to sample new buffets, and compare them to ones we have already tried – so much fun!

We always try to save some money by the following tips below.

Our recommendations? Here are some we swear by!

*Grab a quick, inexpensive breakfast.** We love to start the day with a donut and a coffee. There are many Krispy Kreme and Dunkin Donuts outlets in the resorts. Our favorites include the Krispy Kreme stores in the Excalibur food court and in the one in Circus Circus.

Hit the buffets at lunch! The food is essentially the same, but you will pay less, and can then have a light dinner because you will probably be so stuffed!

Try at least one fun food court. There are very substantial food courts at the following hotels:

Caesars, Excalibur, Four Queens, Harrah's, Luxor, Monte Carlo, New York, New York, Plaza, Venetian**.**

* **Eat at one expensive resort, like Wynn or the Venetian, and try to have lunch there**. The cost is, again, less at lunch, and you can easily split many meals with two guests. We recently ate at an intimate pizzeria at the Grand Canal Shoppes, and split a pizza. This is perfectly fine, and most places will provide you with complimentary bread. Also – share a soda, and keep getting refills.

*For buffets, especially, arrive early to get a good seat**. If the buffet opens at eleven, be sure to be in line ten or so minutes early. This sounds early for lunch, but remember - it's a buffet, so you can take your time, and you will also want to take your time! No one will rush you, and a buffet is a very relaxed and stress-free dining venue.

Strip – Our Recommended Picks

You really can't go too wrong with most cafes and restaurants in on the Vegas strip. Most are good, and many are excellent and cannot be missed. The ones we have detailed truly stand out to us and receive rave reviews. In addition to the ones we list, there are, of course, tons of other options that will suit anyone's budget. We detail several very handy food courts later on this chapter, as well.

BurGR– Planet Hollywood

www.planethollywoodresort.com. 1.702.785.5555. 3677 Las Vegas Blvd. South. Price: Moderate. Cuisine: American. Lunch and dinner.

Famed chef and television personality Gordon Ramsay of Great Britain currently has three eateries in Sin City. BurGr is probably the best of the three, and regularly receives top reviews online. Located right inside the entrance to the thriving Planet Hollywood resort, BurGR has an eclectic but popular menu. The interior is quaint and cozy.

Hearty portions of burgers, fries, and of course – amazing desserts round out this fun and not overly priced menu. The sweet potato and truffle fries, as well as the nice variety of burgers and onion rings are always favorites here. The Farro-Quinoa chicken salad is also a healthy option, and delicious to boot.

Café Bellagio

www.bellagio.com. 1.702.693.7111. 3600 Las Vegas Blvd. South. Cost: Moderate. Cuisine: American. Breakfast, lunch, and dinner.

Overlooking both the Mediterranean-style pool complex and the conservatory and gardens, Cafe Bellagio is really an ideal place to enjoy a meal. Very opulent, the lighting is elegant, and the food definitely matches the setting. Café Bellagio offers a lot of tasty menu options for guests, and the prices are moderate.

Breakfast choices include omelets, pancakes, and even a Bananas foster waffle, which makes us hungry just thinking about this! A prix fixe lunch and dinner menu offers a starter course that includes a daily soup, a main course, and a dessert. Classic American dishes here include lobster mac n cheese, burgers, and salmon. Café Bellagio also has an extensive drink menu that includes fruit smoothies, cappuccinos, and mochas. This place is a great choice for any meal.

Bouchon – Venetian

www.thomaskeller.com. / www.venetian.com. 1.702.414.1000. 3355 Las Vegas Blvd. South. Cost: Very expensive. Cuisine: French. Lunch and dinner.

Famed Thomas Keller is probably the most successful American chef today, and has earned an impressive total of 7 Michelin stars. His French Laundry restaurant near San Francisco is widely considered to be one of the very best restaurants in America, and has 3 Michelin stars, which is the top honor any chef can have. Bouchon, his Las Vegas restaurant and bakery, holds one star, and is also amazing, and a true taste for the senses.

A classic French restaurant, Bouchon provides impeccable service and attention to diners. The setting, in the Venezia tower of the venerable Venetian resort, is simple and elegant. A diverse menu that includes a full oyster bar is a fan favorite, and dishes like the Croque Madame, a ham and cheese sandwich served on brioche bread, are amazing. Fresh bread and butter, a cheese plate, and eggs and omelets for breakfast are also tasty treats.

Canaletto – Venetian

www.grandcanalshoppes.com. 3355 Las Vegas Blvd. South. Price: Moderate. Cuisine: Italian. Lunch and dinner.

One of the many jewels of the Venetian dining scene, Canaletto is perched smack dab in the middle of the charming recreation of Mark's Square, and features great Italian food and desserts. Prices are moderate, and you can easily save some money by going here at lunchtime and/or sharing a pizza.

Wood-fired pizzas, hearty pastas, and Italian desserts like gelato and cannolis round out the menu. We recommend the margherita and pepperoni pizzas. Make sure to request a table overlooking the magic of the square. We recommend getting there early to ensure a prime table for maximum atmosphere and people watching!

Carnegie Deli – Mirage

www.mirage.com. 1.702.791.7111. 3400 Las Vegas Blvd. South. Cost: Moderate. Cuisine: American. Breakfast, lunch, and dinner.

A New York City classic, the Carnegie Deli is still going strong in Manhattan, and the deli in the Mirage is also very popular and well-renowned. Located right inside the casino, the Carnegie Deli serves huge, overstuffed sandwiches, soups, burgers and great desserts. Several popular sandwiches include the hot pastrami, roast beef, and turkey club. Carnegie's is also known for their delicious soups, including its' famous matzo ball soup, and there are great burgers on the menu, here, as well.

Desserts like chocolate chip cookies, apple pie, and carrot cake are crowd pleasers. This deli is not cheap - be prepared to spend upwards of $15 or so on your meal, per person, but the ambience of an all-American diner and the tasty food make the prices worth it.

Our Pick: The Cheesecake Factory – The Forum Shops, Caesar's Palace

www.caesarspalace.com. 1.702.731.7710. 3570 Las Vegas Blvd. South. Price: Moderate. Cuisine: American. Breakfast, lunch, and dinner.

An American favorite, we had to include The Cheesecake Factory in this chapter because it is so darn tasty! You will often hear that restaurants aren't supposed to have menus as big as the one at the Cheesecake, but it works here, because everything is so good!

The menu is simply chock full of everything from pizzas, burgers, burritos, and, of course, a myriad of tantalizing cheesecake choices for dessert. Our pick? The nachos appetizer is mouth-watering and huge, and will easily fill up two people. The free bread and butter platter they serve here also hits the spot, and is essentially a free appetizer. The small plates are also a great way to go, and ordering two or three can easily make a meal, especially when combined with the bevy of free bread.

Desserts here, of course, are legendary, and no visit is complete without at least thinking of ordering one of their cheesecakes. Over twenty different varieties are sold, but we recommend the classic plain version, and make sure to have it come adorned with strawberries.

The Grand Lux Café – Venetian

www.venetian.com. 1.702. 414.1000. 3355 Las Vegas Blvd. South. Price: Moderate. Cuisine: American. Breakfast, lunch, and dinner.

Owned by the same company that owns and manages its sister eatery, The Cheesecake Factory, The Grand Lux Café also has a wide variety of dishes to choose from. Set in an open, pleasing space, this café will probably remind you of the Cheesecake Factory, but the look here is more casual and not nearly as splashy.

Favorite dishes here include tasty pizzas, nachos, and burgers. Much like its sister restaurant, The Grand Lux Café serves similar food, and we recommend the all-American favorites like the nachos, burgers, and burritos. Desserts are not too pricey, and include sundaes, cheesecake, and a selection of freshly baked pies.

Joel Robuchon – MGM Grand

www.mgmgrand.com. 1.702.891.7777. 3799 Las Vegas Blvd. South. Price: Very expensive. Cuisine: French. Dinner only.

Joel Robuchon is a legendary French chef, known for his culinary expertise, and his amazing restaurant at the MGM Grand is upscale and posh. Robuchon was born and raised in France, and rose to fame there, and his signature restaurant is the only Michelin three-star award winning Vegas restaurant. He holds 30 Michelin stars, and is currently the highest ranked Michelin chef in the world.

If you are not familiar with the Michelin system, this is the highest dining award in the world, and a huge honor. Even one star is a big deal! Clearly, Robuchon knows what he's doing, and his decadent and expertly prepared food reflects this fact.

This restaurant is exquisite, with an expansive garden terrace in Art Deco style, and marble floors. Robuchon also has another restaurant at the MGM Grand, L'Atelier, and this is also a very ritzy dining experience. Busy with his other worldwide restaurants, there are several chefs in-residence here, and are they amazing, as well! Robuchon is known for upscale French cuisine, including caviar, frog legs fritters, scallops, and salmon.

As ritzy as this is, it is not a snobby experience, but do be prepared to pay at least $150 per person for their Prix Fixe menu. Desserts like the sumptuous mango and passion fruit sorbet will leave your mouth watering for more

Our Pick : Mon Ami Gabi – Paris

www.parislasvegas.com. 1.702. 944.4224. 3655 Las Vegas Blvd. South (in Paris Las Vegas). Price: Moderate. Cuisine: French. Lunch and dinner.

A classic French café can be found at Paris Las Vegas. Mon Ami Gabi offers breakfast, lunch, brunch, and dinner menus, but whatever meal you choose, be sure to be seated outdoors if you can. The views of the Bellagio and its' fountains are spectacular, and it's always fun to sit and people watch in Las Vegas.

All three meals are served here, and breakfasts especially are amazing, and oh so French! The fresh crepes melt in your mouth, and waffles are another smart choice. A brunch menu is also available on select days. Lunches and dinner menus feature fish, sandwiches, steak frites, freshly baked bread, and a classic French cheese plate.

Save some room for dessert, at Mon Ami Gabi, which stands for "My Friend Gabi" by the way. Here, you can choose from selections such as crème brulee and chocolate mousse. This place is a winner, and always a fan favorite in Vegas.

Paradise Café – Mirage

www.mirage.com. 1.702.791.7111. 3400 Las Vegas Blvd. South. Cost: Moderate. Cuisine: American. Breakfast and lunch.

Open seasonally, the Paradise Café is open from 9 am to 3 pm. The café is located next to the pool area, and open to both Mirage guests and visitors. The lush greenery, palm trees, and views of the pool complex are amazing as you nosh on all-American food and the all-day breakfast menu. Guests sit under colorful umbrellas on wicker chairs, and tables are marble-topped – very classy!

The all-day breakfast menu includes made-to-order omelettes, eggs, and Paradise toast, which is a mouth-watering chocolate brioche topped with coconut whipped cream, powdered sugar and maple syrup – oh my! Other favorites here include burgers, salads, and great coffee and Bloody Marys. This place is a treat to eat at – very casual and great food.

Picasso – Bellagio

www.bellagio.com. 1.702.693.7111. 3600 Las Vegas Blvd. South. Price: Very expensive. Cuisine: French and European. Dinner only.

Picasso is a fascinating restaurant, we promise you that! Where else can you dine under, literally, millions of dollars of actual Picasso paintings that hang on the walls? Spaniard Pablo Picasso was an amazing painter, and the food here, inspired by him, is also amazing and superbly presented. This is one of the top restaurants in all of Las Vegas, and the menu and gracious service will quickly tell you why.

Chef Julian Serrano is very well-known for his cuisine, which is European-inspired - French, specifically. Open only for dinner, dishes like poached oysters and New Zealand snapper, along with veal chops, are all great options.

There is also a Prix Fixe menu, which covers appetizers, the main course, and dessert. An extensive wine cellar is also found at Picasso, with a whopping 1,500 different selections. Prices are very steep, and can climb to over $200 for two people, but if you can afford it, Picasso is definitely worth every penny!

The Pyramid Café – Luxor

www.luxor.com. 1.702.262.4000. 2900 Las Vegas Blvd. South. Cost: Moderate. Cuisine: American. Breakfast and lunch.

Situated smack dab in the heart of the cool, atmospheric Luxor casino, the Pyramid Café is a classic Las Vegas diner. Great, hearty portions of American food are served here, and the bill won't break your budget.

The breakfasts here are very popular with patrons, with entrees like omelets, pancakes, Orange Creamsicle French toast, and Churros Waffles. This is a fun way to start the day, and is very affordable.

Lunches include the Western BBQ burger and the Philly Steak sandwich. Be sure to check out the extensive drink selection, as well, and to take some time to explore the Luxor after or before your tasty meal.

Rainforest Café – Planet Hollywood.

www.rainforestcafe.com. 1.702.891.8580. 3717 Las Vegas Blvd South (in Planet Hollywood). Cost: Moderate. Cuisine: American. Lunch and dinner.

An American favorite, the Rainforest Café serves lunch and dinner, and used to be situated in MGM Grand, but has moved to Planet Hollywood to set up permanent residence. If you've never been to a Rainforest Café, they specialize in American food and the setting is a virtual recreation of (you guessed it!) - a rainforest. Noisy "parrots" and other rainforest animals can be heard as you sit amongst fake trees and lush foliage. The effect is festive, and noisy, but great fun, especially for kids.

Service is great, and the food is good – not always great, but certainly worth a lunch or dinner here. The Rainforest Café specializes in burgers, pasta, chicken dishes, and a great selection of desserts. A huge retail shop is right outside the restaurant, and features a nice selection of apparel, stuffed animals, and educational books.

Steakhouse at Camelot – Excalibur

www.excalibur.com. 1.702.597.7700. 3850 Las Vegas Blvd. South. Cost: Expensive. Cuisine: American. Lunch and dinner.

Pricey but a great value, this upscale restaurant is loved by guest for its' tasty American dishes and elegant decor. Located in the fun, Medieval theme Excalibur, the Steakhouse at Camelot is a colorful, yet sedate choice for an all-American meal. The décor is simple and elegant, and the service is attentive and gracious.

 A wide variety of steaks, Caesar salads and seafood are the big draws here. An extensive wine list is available, and the Steakhouse also serves many amazing desserts like New York-style cheesecake, ice cream, vanilla crème brulee, and tiramisu.

Stripside Café and Bar – Caesars Palace.

www.caesars.com. 1.702.731.7710. 3570 Las Vegas Blvd. South. Cost: Moderate. Cuisine: American.

Now that the fun Serendipity 3 has closed, the Stripside Café and Bar has taken its' place, overlooking the Strip and occupying a prime spot of real estate. Right outside Caesars Palace, this café is a fun spot to grab some tasty all-American food like burgers, onion rings, fries, and chicken parmesan. Their nachos are also huge, and delicious.

Breakfast which includes dishes like the massive and tasty huevos rancheros burritos, is served all day. Tasty milkshakes like cookies and cream, sundaes, and ice cream are very popular at Stripside, and will add that dash of sugar you may need to keep up your energy in this town.

SW Steakhouse – Wynn

www.wynnlasvegas.com. 1.702.770.7100. 3131 Las Vegas Blvd. South. Cost: Expensive. Cuisine: American. Lunch and dinner.

With views of the stunning Wynn Lake of Dreams, SW Steakhouse is a romantic and atmospheric place to enjoy a meal. No, this isn't a cheap meal by any standard, but the food and surroundings are worth the prices. Chef David Walzog is well-known for his meals in this four-star award-winning eatery. He cooks up tasty dishes like a double ribeye steak, fresh oysters, and foie gras.

There is also a vegetarian menu, as well, which you don't see in all restaurants. Sides include a homemade mac and cheese and wild sautéed mushrooms. SW Steakhouse is a very popular restaurant for sure, with all-American dining at its' best. Take some time also to wander the wonderful Wynn resort after or before you dine – it's worth your time.

Top of the World Restaurant

www.stratosphere.com. 1.702.380.7777. 2000 Las Vegas Blvd. South. Cost: Very expensive. Cuisine: American. Lunch and dinner.

Situated 800 feet above the Earth, Top of the World is a restaurant that rotates a full 360 degrees every 80 minutes as you dine. Very cool, right?

Amazing views of the Strip and also the thrill-seekers who are bungee jumping beside you, at the Stratosphere's thrill rides, are just some of the cool bonuses of eating here. This place is very popular and a romantic spot, as well, so we recommend making a reservation.

Open for lunch and dinner, there is a fixed-price menu for each meal, and you can also order a la carte. The $49 fixed prix meal for lunch includes your choice of a salad, fish for the main course and a dessert, like crème brulee. Dinner's prix fixe menu is $98 and offers 4 courses of dishes like lobster, steak, seared Maine scallops, and foie gras – very gourmet. This place is a winner, and a special place to dine with that special someone.

Off-Strip dining

Many of the most wonderful restaurants can be found off-Strip, and many tourists tend to stick to the comfort of the Strip, but venture out! Hop in a taxi and explore this city, which is just teeming with amazing dining spots. We will detail our favorites here, as well as some of the most well-renowned hot spots in Vegas.

Alize – The Palms

www.alize.com. 1.702.951.7000. 4321 West Flamingo Rd, Las Vegas. Cost: Expensive. Cuisine: French. Lunch and dinner.

A classic French restaurant, Alize is located at the top of the party-hard resort, the Palms, which is a bit ironic! A sedate, gorgeous restaurant in this resort? Go figure, right? Well, Alize is very gourmet and romantic, and a place that consistently receives rave reviews on tripadvisor.com. A prix five menu called the Chef's Tasting menu covers 7 courses, and is expensive, at over $100 a person, but worth every penny, in our opinion!

Dishes like scallops, lamb and foie gras are good bets, and Alize also features many specialty drinks, and is also known for their extensive wine selection. Desserts like chocolate raspberry macaroons with espresso mocha sauce make my mouth water even as I write this! Alize is a winner, and most guests who visit come again and again.

Cadillac Mexican Kitchen and Tequila Bar

www.goldennugget.com. 1.702.386.8169. 129 Fremont Street. Cost: Moderate. Cuisine: Mexican. Lunch and dinner.

A staple at the Golden Nugget, this Mexican eatery shines for not only its' mouth-watering food but also for really great service. TVs pepper this modern eatery, and create the feel of a hip sports bar that attracts guests and visitors, as well as plenty of locals. Yes, this place is that good!

Dishes like fajita shrimp tacos, nachos, chicken taquitos, and veggie tacos are all winners. As the name suggests, there is a wide variety of tequilas, margaritas, and other drinks. A daily happy hour offers great deals on meals and drinks, and the rocking bar is always hopping at the Cadillac Mexican Kitchen.

Culinary Dropout – Hard Rock Resort

www.culinarydropout.com. 1.702.693.5000. 4455 Paradise Rd. Las Vegas. Cost: Moderate. Cuisine: American. Lunch and dinner.

Located at the hip, trendy Hard Rock Resort, Culinary Dropout, even with its' name, also a hip and trendy place to eat. The décor is trendy and modern, and the staff is usually very gracious. The clientele is a nice mixture of young and old, and many locals love this place!

This place receives consistent rave reviews, and the food will tell you why. American favorites like burgers, the bistro steak, BBQ pork belly nachos, and rainbow trout are all favorites. Staff "mixologists" prepare a wide variety of drinks for happy guests. Try the bacon bloody mary if you dare!

Culinary Dropout is always rocking well into the evening and early morning hours, and definitely caters to those who enjoy a boisterous dining experience.

Hofbrauhaus

www.hofbrauhaus.com. 1.702.853.BEER (2337). 4510 Paradise Rd. Las Vegas. Cost: Moderate. Cuisine: German. Lunch and dinner.

Opa! Welcome to Hofbrauhaus, a bastion of German food and culture on the west side of the Strip. Within walking distance of the Strip (albeit a long walk), this is a fun and festive eatery that will transport you straight to the legendary and classic beer halls of Germany.

This entire restaurant is a local institution, and is modeled after a Munich beer hall, or "beir hall". Sexy beer maidens will actually spank you as you take a shot!, and you can also play games such as Beer Pong and musical chairs. No, this is not your typical restaurant, right?

Menu favorites include classic German dishes like potato pancakes, Bavarian potato soup, freshly baked pretzels, and a mixed cheese plate. We recommend the cheese plater, which has many different varieties of cheese that you don't find everywhere. Obviously, there is a plethora of different types of beers, but you really need to try the authentic German beers on tap.

Hugo's Cellar – Four Queens

www.hugoscellar.com. 1.702.385.4011. Cost: Expensive. Cuisine: French and American. Lunch and dinner.

Hugo's Cellar is a cozy, intimate restaurant located deep within the venerable Four Queens resort in downtown Las Vegas. Muck like the Four Queens itself, Hugo's Cellar is a more sedate place to go, and you will find many Vegas locals who frequent this place on a regular basis.

A consistent winner of the Las Vegas Review's "Best Gourmet Room", Hugo's Cellar always usually receives rave reviews from guests and critics alike. Each female diner receives a red rose during the meal, which is a sweet touch.

The menu features all sorts of dishes, such as lobster bisque soup, escargots, and shrimp cocktail. A wide variety of meats are available, and very pricey: $76 for a 10 oz. steak with bacon! Desserts are also quite tasty, and you can nosh on items like bananas foster, which is so fresh and delicious.

Metro Pizza

www.metropizza.com. 1.702.736.1955. 1395 East Tropicana Ave., Las Vegas. Cost: Inexpensive. Cuisine: Italian. Lunch and dinner.

Metro Pizza, with 4 locations in Las Vegas, and one in nearby Henderson, is widely known in Las Vegas as having some of the best New York-style pizza in town. This thinner style of pizza, famous in the Big Apple, is delicious here, and Metro serves affordable pies, delicious garlic knots with marinara sauce, and fresh salads. They also offer complimentary Italian bread for each guest.

Bright, colorful murals line the walls of each eatery, helping to make Metro is a nice place to grab a cheap, tasty meal. Perhaps the best-known location in Vegas is the restaurant on East Tropicana Avenue, not too far from the MGM Grand. A little out of the way, the pizza, sides, and attentive, friendly service are worth the detour for many visitors.

Oscar's Steakhouse – Plaza Hotel

www.plazahotelcasino.com. 1.800.634.6575. 1 Main Street, Las Vegas. Cost: Moderate. Cuisine: American.

The former, very flamboyant Las Vegas mayor Oscar B. Goodman, who was well-loved by his constituents, opened this restaurant a few years back at the classy Plaza Hotel. Located in the heart of Fremont Street, and overlooking the street itself, this steakhouse is known for its' amazing steaks, salads, and fresh sides like mac 'n cheese. Oscar's also boasts a very extensive and fun bar that serves Goodman's favorite drink, a martini, and many, many other tasty libations.

A fun thing about Oscar's is that "broads", who are really beautiful and outgoing hostesses, will come to your table and chat it up with you. They appeal, of course, to single men, and are a very unique attribute to this already unique eatery. The restaurant itself is very upscale, with huge chandeliers overlooking the room, and windows that overlook all the action on the always bustling Fremont Street.

Pamplemousse

www.pamplemousserestaurant.com. 1.702.733.2066. 400 East Sahara Ave, Las Vegas. Cost: Moderate. Cuisine: French. Lunch and dinner.

Pamplemousse is a word that means "grapefruit" in French. This eclectic restaurant is a local favorite, and features a very unusual menu. Located on the east side of the Strip, on Sahara Avenue, this place has been going strong since 1976, and is a favorite with locals and guests alike. The exterior is very unassuming, but the interior is decorated simply and tastefully, with framed photographs and art posters. Soft music and low lighting make this a nice spot for a romantic meal.

Famous for its' French cuisine such as escargot, salmon, and wild mushroom ravioli, Pamplemousse also features a fixe prix menu. Much like other restaurants that offer this type of menu, here you receive a set number of courses, either four or five, and pay a set price. The value here is enormous – these prix fixe menus start at $40 and up.

Desserts such as mousse and crème brulee round out the menu, and help to top off a great meal.

Buffets

You came to Las Vegas to experience a great buffet? Well, you are not alone. Most guests come to experience all that this city has to offer, and the whole idea of a buffet is pretty much synonymous with Las Vegas. Yes, there are some lackluster buffets in this city, but in our experience, most are amazing, and you get a lot of bang for your buck. Even cheaper buffets, like the ones found at smaller hotels like Gold *Coast and Sam's Town, offer better food than you may think.*

Cost is not correlated to quality – we cannot stress this enough!

Don't be afraid to try a cheaper buffet because you're worried that the food will be mediocre – often times, it's the opposite. Also, make sure you come either early or late to a buffet, as lines can be brutal in Vegas, especially for the most popular buffets.

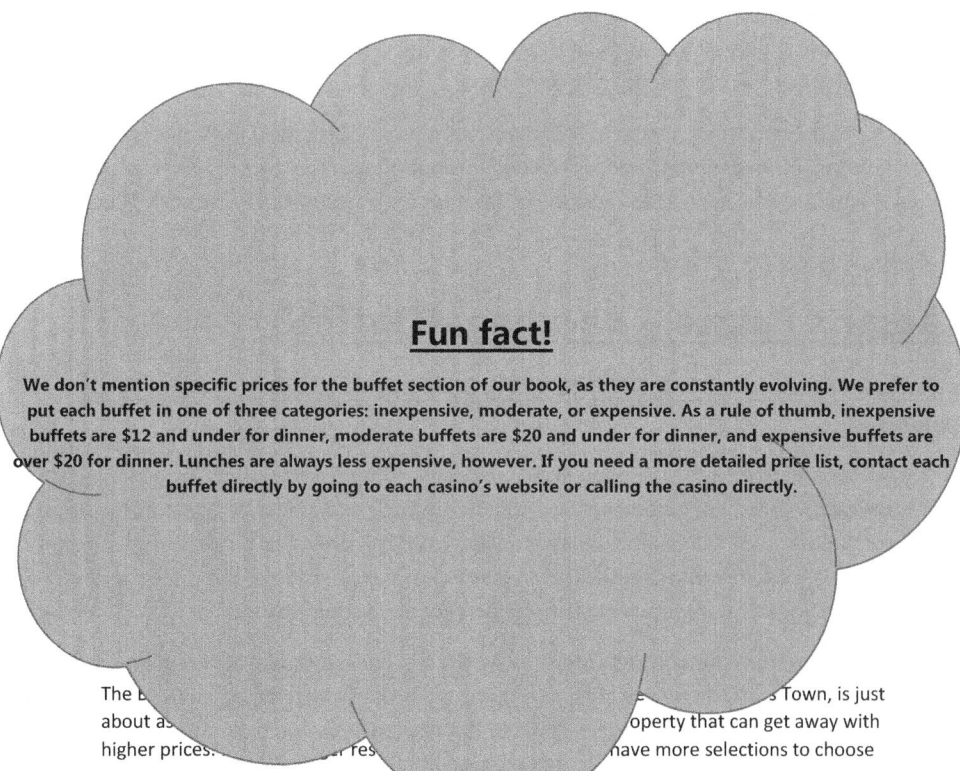

Fun fact!

We don't mention specific prices for the buffet section of our book, as they are constantly evolving. We prefer to put each buffet in one of three categories: inexpensive, moderate, or expensive. As a rule of thumb, inexpensive buffets are $12 and under for dinner, moderate buffets are $20 and under for dinner, and expensive buffets are over $20 for dinner. Lunches are always less expensive, however. If you need a more detailed price list, contact each buffet directly by going to each casino's website or calling the casino directly.

The b   Town, is just
about a   operty that can get away with
higher prices.   res   have more selections to choose

from, and are more elegantly appointed. The food quality, however, is often the same or very similar.

Our Picks for the best buffets....

Bellagio

www.bellagio.com. 1.702.693.7111. 3600 Las Vegas Blvd. South. Cost: Expensive.

You will pay for your meal at Bellagio's Buffet, that's for sure! What you will get in return for your money, though, is definitely worth every penny. Mouth-watering pizza, Mexican, Italian, and other stations, plus a huge array of desserts, including sugar-free selections tempt guests. The smells alone are worth the price of admission!

One of the pricier buffets in town, Bellagio is still a great bet, especially if this is your first buffet in Vegas. A sleek, modern décor defines this buffet, and the décor is sleek and the seating is ample. Make sure to arrive early or later, as major lines form very early here!

Caesar's Palace – Bacchanal Buffet

www.caesarspalace.com. 1.702.731.7710. 3570 Las Vegas Blvd. South. Price: Expensive.

This buffet, unfortunately, wins the award for one of the priciest buffets in town – no small feat! Fortunately for visitors, however, the food is amazing and ample, and seems to please most guests. Caesar's is full of amazing restaurants, and this one is no different. Your wallet may be hurting a bit after the family takes in this buffet, (at press time, the price for dinner was a whopping $55!) but your stomach will likely be very happy, and stuffed!

As you can see from the photo of the candied apples, the Bacchanal buffet spares no expense for its food offerings, and the price matches this! The interior is paneled in brick, and diners can see the wood-fired ovens burning in the background. The experience is upscale, modern, and fun. Lines are long, to be expected, so get here early.

The Bacchanal Buffet is sleek and modern, and offers many different stations, such as Asian, Italian, and Mexican. The dessert selection is also extensive, and offers many traditional and ksugar-free offerings.

Gold Coast Ports o' Call Buffet

www.goldcoastcasino.com. 1.702.367.7111. 4000 West Flamingo Rd., Las Vegas. Cost: Inexpensive.

A smaller buffet, the Ports of Call buffet is proof that, as we stated, cost is not correlated to quality. The food here is fresh, abundant, and a great value. With prices never raising above $15 a person, you can eat for cheap here, and not even realize that the food is every bit as good as most buffets on the Strip that are a lot more expensive.

Ports 'O call offers a wide medley of food stations, and a huge variety of desserts. A fun Friday seafood buffet is also available, and serves, among other items, very fresh crabs, shrimp, and oysters. This buffet is also known for its' made-to-order eggs and omelets for breakfast and for friendly, attentive service.

Main Street Station – Garden Court Buffet

www.mainstreetstation.com. 1.702.387.1896. 200 North Main Street, Las Vegas. Cost: Inexpensive.

Located inside the smaller, quaint resort and casino, Main Street Station, in the heart of downtown Vegas, is one of the best buffets in town. Set in a pretty space with many flowers, The Garden Court Buffet is an amazing value, as well. For half of what you would pay at many Strip buffets, this buffet offers essentially the same quality of food and presentation.

On our last visit here, we were impressed by the ample dessert selection, and the fresh, hot pizza station. Lines form here very early for all three meals, because of the great value and extensive offerings here. For under $10, you will get a very filling lunch, and dinner is never more than $12 a person, making this a steal!

*Our pick: More: The Buffet at Luxor

www.luxor.com. 1.702.262.4000. 2900 Las Vegas Blvd. South. Cost: Moderate.

More: The Buffet at Luxor is a fun place to gorge yourself on a tantalizing spread of food. The theme here, like the Luxor itself, is a fun Egyptian one, and the space is a great one in which to enjoy a meal.

Much like the other buffets we discuss, More has a great variety of food stations to explore. A handy wood-fired pizza station and an amazing dessert selection are here, as well. Locals and visitors who visit this buffet love to tell you that the price to quality ratio is very high here. In other words, you get a lot for your money here.

Lines tend to be long here, so come either early or late, when the crowds have dissipated a bit. Breakfast is also a good bet, when the lines are a bit shorter.

Mirage – Cravings Buffet

www.mirage.com. 1.702.791.7111. 3400 Las Vegas Blvd. South. Cost: Expensive.

A somewhat stark buffet, Cravings features a modern look, which is a little strange considering that it's located inside a very tropical hotel, the Mirage. Well, no one's perfect, right?

Most likely, you will enjoy the wide variety of food stations, and the unlimited beer and wine bar is a winner, as is the amazing selection of desserts, including sugar-free options. A great champagne brunch is popular here that serves unlimited drinks, including wines and mimosas.

A carving station with fresh duck, ham, turkey, and prime rib will please the meat-eater in your party, and Cravings, like many other buffets, also offers several gluten-free options, as well.

Paris – The Village Buffet

www.parislasvegas.com. 1.702.946.7000. 3655 Las Vegas Blvd. South. Cost: Moderate to Expensive.

Love Paris and France in general? Then you've come to the right place! Set in a very cozy French village-style space, The Village Buffet boasts, among other stations, their fan-favorite crepe station. Guests here enjoy hot, fresh, made-to-order crepes that are very popular in Paris. If you have not tried one, try one here for the first time – they are that good. Other tasty breakfast offerings include omelets and fresh-squeezed fruit juices.

Both French and American dishes are popular here, so whatever your taste, you will probably enjoy this buffet. Food is fresh and tasty, and this buffet is a treat to behold. Fresh fish, like salmon and crab legs, are available, and desserts like crème brulee are homemade. Make sure to either come early or late, as lines form very quickly here – the word is out with how great this buffet is.

Rio – Seafood Buffet & World Buffet

www.riolasvegas.com. 1.702.777.7777. 3700 West Flamingo Rd, Las Vegas. Cost: Expensive.

Yes, this is a two-for-one buffet! On most nights, this is a huge buffet, with the traditional offerings combined with a major seafood element. To be honest, we have heard that the quality has gone down in recent years, which is too bad, because Rio's massive buffet has both won many awards in Las Vegas for their quality and quantity. We still recommend this buffet, however, especially if you are a huge seafood lover.

The regular buffet has an amazing array of dishes and different international stations - hence the name "World Buffet". The seafood portion features a great selection of seafood items, including fresh lobster, crabs, and oysters. The modern design of this buffet is a pleaser, and its' location in the fun Rio resort and casino makes it even more enjoyable a place to partake a meal in, as you have a perfect excuse to explore when you are done!

Sam's Town Firelight Buffet – Top Pick

www.samstown.com. 1.702.456.7777. 5111 Boulder Hwy, Las Vegas. Cost: Inexpensive.

One of our favorite buffets in the world, Sam's Town is so good that you almost not believe what you are *not* spending on this buffet. Breakfast and lunch and dinner are all at or under $10 a person, and this beautiful, abundant buffet with tasty, fresh cuisine pleases most guests.

Very reminiscent of a larger buffet on the Strip, the Firelight Buffet is grouped into different stations, and we were amazed by the sheer variety of food offered, especially the desserts. Like other way more pricey buffets, the many stations, like Mexican and Italian, are here, including fresh, tasty pizza.

The décor is sleek and modern, and the staff is warm and friendly. The experience at Sam's Firelight Buffet is simply a delight. You must take some time to explore this unique, self-contained resort after your buffet.

Our pick: Wynn buffet

www.wynnlasvegas.com. 1.702.770.7100. 3131 Las Vegas Blvd. South. Cost: Very expensive.

Just wander into this opulent buffet, and you will see why guests readily fork over $20 for lunch, and over $30 for dinner. This is an over the top buffet experience with food to die for. The fresh flowers and bright colors welcome you in, and the amount of food available almost overwhelmed us, to be honest!

The Wynn even offers a cheese station, which is pretty rare in Vegas, as well as the standard ethnic stations, like Mexican and Italian. There are huge lines here, so arrive early or be prepared to wait.

Much like other buffets, the Wynn offers multiple stations, and the desserts will make you so happy you may have to have two of three! Sugar free selections, of course, abound here, and make for a buffet that will most likely please everyone in your party.

Sweet Treats – Places to Get Your Sugar Fix!

Yes, Vegas has it all, folks. Legendary, posh eateries, famous buffets, food courts, and, of course, plenty of places to go into a near sugar shock. But, c'mon – you are on vacation! You will probably end up walking several miles a day, especially with the vast casinos, right? The funny thing is, there actually is a great deal of walking that goes on in Vegas. Even if you take the monorail or another shuttle, you will inevitably walk several miles a day in the casinos and malls alone.

Treat yourself then to a decadent box of chocolates, a tasty cappuccino, or some creamy sorbet or gelato. Like any fun tourist spot, Las Vegas has plenty of eateries designed specifically to make you a fan of all things sugar. Come explore these winners!

Bouchon – Venetian

www.venetian.com. 1.702.414.1000. 3355 Las Vegas Blvd. South. Cost: Moderate.

Bouchon is the brain child of famed restaurant owner Thomas Keller, who owns several award-winning French restaurants in America, including one in the Venetian. This bakery is a much smaller version of that eatery, and is located at the Venezia tower, right opposite a bank of elevators.

As you can imagine, Bouchon receives long lines at times, and offers a wide selection of goodies, such as macaroons, café au lait, croissants, and muffins. The pastries and other items are baked oh so fresh, and it's a fun spot for a daily sugar fix while in Vegas! Be sure to also check out their extensive selection of coffees and drinks.

Café Belle Madeleine – Paris

www.parislasvegas.com. 1.702.946.7000. 3655 Las Vegas Blvd. South. Cost: Moderate.

In the mood for a classic French pastry? Then look no further! Head to Café Belle Madeleine, in the heart of the Paris shopping arcade. Very close to the casino, Paris boasts this cute, quaint café that is a great spot for a light lunch or a sweet treat. This café is a set up as a classic French bakery, or boulangerie, and it serves quiche, tarts, croissants, pastries, cupcakes, cookies, coffee drinks, and gelato.

French-inspired treats like chocolate raspberry mousse and chocolate eclairs are also a great bet. Shopper take note – you can take home a nice, French-inspired souvenir here, and you can also purchase boxes of cupcakes and Godiva chocolates. Tres delicieux!

Carlo's Bake Shop – Venetian

www.venetian.com. 1.702.414.1000. 3355 Las Vegas Blvd. South. Cost: Moderate.

Yes, this is the famous Carlo's Bake Shop from the popular show "Cake Boss"! We first saw this place and we knew it would be amazing, and it is! Buddy and his family have come to the Venetian, and this amazing bakery is located just off the Grand Canal Shoppes, at the Venetian resort.

Like their other locations, Carlo's offers a tantalizing selection of bakery favorites like peanut butter cupcakes, cannolis, donuts, chocolate-covered strawberries, and a great selection of drinks, as well. Lines can be long here, as the quality is so high, so plan accordingly. This is a great place to grab a coffee and a pastry after you shop your heart out at the Grand Canal Shoppes.

Crepe Expectations

www.crepeexpectations.com. 1.702.583.4939. 9500 South East Ave., Ste 150, Las Vegas. Cost: Inexpensive.

As you might guess, this fun eatery, located on the East of the Strip, on Sahara Avenue, specializes in tasty, fresh crepes. This place is small and can become crowded at meal times, as the news has gotten out that their crepes are delicious. Open from 9 am to 3 pm, come here for a great and unique breakfast or lunch.

A crepe, by the way, if you are new to this food, is a pastry that completely encloses a filling, such as bananas, strawberries, or even lunch meats. Each dish here, which includes sandwiches, such as tuna and turkey, is actually a crepe.

Numerous flavors, included banana and the popular Nutella, are all mouth-watering, and there are dozens of choices for your crepe. A nice selection of wine and coffee drinks are available, as well, for your enjoyment.

Drugstore Café – Wynn

www.wynnlasvegas.com. 1.702.770.7100. 3131 Las Vegas Blvd. South. Cost: Moderate.

Many visitors to Vegas, and even to the Wynn may easily overlook this gem, but you shouldn't if you want a great snack in a cozy locale. Part eatery and part bakery, the Drugstore Café is a great place to grab one of the endless pastries, and muffins. The café also sells many drinks, such as cappuccino, mocha, and coffee.

Part of the fun of this café is where it is actually located – in the Wynn Resort, which is simply fun to stroll around in with your coffee or pastry from the Drugstore Café.

Espressamente Illy - Palazzo

www.palazzo.com. 1.702.414.1000. 3355 Las Vegas Blvd. South. Cost: Moderate.

Located inside the charming and upscale Palazzo resort, The Drugstore Café features fresh sandwiches, espresso, coffee drinks, and breakfast pastries. Be sure to fuel up here before exploring the beautiful resort that is the Wynn Las Vegas. We especially recommend the enticing coffee drinks and cappuccino.

Very cozy inside, Espressamente Illy is an eatery and bakery serving all sorts of meals and sweet treats. Breakfast, lunch, and dinner are served, and Illy focuses on authentic, Italian pizzas, sandwiches, coffee, baked goods, and gelato. The coffee is amazing – you must try some on your visit to Illy at the Palazzo. This is one of those places that you'll end up coming to several times – it's that good!

Ghirardelli Ice Cream and Chocolate Shop – Linq

www.ghirardelli.com. 1.702.650.0096. 3545 Las Vegas Blvd. South. Cost: Moderate.

The famous San-Francisco based Ghirardelli chocolate shops are known worldwide for their freshly made shakes, ice cream, and small tasty squares of chocolate. This location, just one of many, is located in the very pleasant Linq outdoor shopping promenade.

You will often find a line of people, queuing up for shakes, boxes of chocolates, and pieces of chocolate. This shop also has a nice selection of ice creams and specialty drinks, including lattes and cappuccinos.

This is the perfect place for a bit of sugar that will give you some energy for your busy day in Las Vegas.

Jean-Phillipe Patisserie – Bellagio

www.bellagio.com. 1.702.693.7111. 3600 Las Vegas Blvd. South. Cost: Moderate.

There is certainly not a shortage of places in the Bellagio to treat yourself to some amazing food. Patisserie is a French word for pastry shop, and this patisserie is a very popular spot for breakfast and treats and drinks all day long. Located inside the Bellagio, you may encounter a line here at any time of the day – yes, it's that good!

This pastry shop/bakery is consistently ranked in the top five bakeries in Vegas on TripAdvisor. A cool, massive chocolate fountain adorns one wall of this eatery, and treats like chocolate-covered strawberries, macaroons, tarts, cakes, and ice cream round out the menu. A myriad of coffees and specialty drinks are also found at Jean-Philippe Patisserie.

Krispy Kreme - Circus Circus, Excalibur, Plaza, Treasure Island

www.krispykreme.com. **Cost: Inexpensive.**

Ok, we are a huge fan of those delicious, sinful donuts, so we had to include this in our sweets section! Krispy Kreme donuts along with a coffee are a great way to start the day. We make it our personal tradition to start each day on our visits to Las Vegas with some coffee and a Krispy Kreme donut. Remember, you are on vacation! You deserve at least one, or maybe two (they are small!). Krispy Kreme also offers a nice selection of coffee and specialty drinks, as well as soft drinks. We recommend the raspberry-filled ones – they are to die for!

Palio – Bellagio

www.bellagio.com. 1.702.693.7111. 3600 Las Vegas Blvd. South. Cost: Moderate

This delightful café and bakery is located near the entrance of Bellagio's expansive pool complex. Palio is a great place to catch a sandwich and a cappuccino on the way to the pool.

For non-guests, this is a nice pit stop to relax, rest your feet and nosh on freshly squeezed orange juice, gelato, sandwiches, or a sugary treat. A huge variety of freshly-made drinks, including coffees and cappuccinos are also served, and will help fuel your day in Vegas.

Payard Patisserie – Caesar's Palace

www.caesarspalace.com. **1.702.731.7710. 3570 Las Vegas Blvd. South. Cost: Moderate.**

Payard's Patisserie is similar to Palio at Bellagio, but there is more emphasis here on chocolate. Prices are a bit high (remember – you are in Caesar's Palace), and the food and chocolates are of very high caliber. If you've ever been to a Godiva chocolate store, Payard's feels very much the same.

Creamy, Italian gelato is legendary here, and the boxes and samples of chocolates are worth the hefty prices. Sandwiches and sides are also available, as well as a nice selection of drinks such as cappuccino, coffee, and specialty coffee drinks.

Sugar Factory – Planet Hollywood

www.planethollywoodresort.com. 1.702.866.0777. 3666 Las Vegas Blvd. South. Cost: Moderate.

The Sugar Factory is known for, yes, you guessed it - sugar! All sorts of sugar, in fact. Coffees, cappuccino, gelato, and a vast selection of candy is available at this cute shop at Planet Hollywood, which is smack dab in the center of all the action on the Strip. This is the place to not only grab a tasty treat for you and a loved one, but also a great souvenir to take home for the ones you love.

Numerous celebrities over the years, like Britney Spears, have endorsed this place. The Sugar Factory's signature lollipops, called couture pops, are all the rage, but will cost you at least $8 a pop! A trendy and affordable restaurant here also features American comfort food like burgers and sandwiches, and the food is very good here, as well.

Chapter 7

Casino Games & Casinos to Explore

Casinos are a dime a dozen in Las Vegas, but there are certainly ones that stand out, and that need to be explored. Whether on or off the Strip, your best bet is to stop by and simply check out each one that looks like fun. Many will surprise you! Many are truly massive, like the casino at MGM Grand, and some are tiny, like the quaint Four Queens in downtown. We personally prefer moderate sized casinos, such as Bellagio and Monte Carlo. Come explore these gems!

Many casinos offer free lessons, and don't hesitate to take one – they are fun and you will be joined by many other novices like you! Understanding better how to play certain games will probably make playing a real game a lot less stressful!

Check out these helpful websites that will guide you through these games, and more!

*www.vegas.com

*www.wikipedia.com

*www.wizardofodds.com

The Games – a Lowdown

Blackjack

Blackjack is the most popular table game in both Vegas casinos and the entire casino world, and for good reason. The whole point of this game, otherwise known as "21", is to be the closest to 21 without going over. Yes, you are playing against the dealer, who, we assume, is going to be a lot more knowledgeable about the game than you are! This is a game of skill, however, unlike many other casino games, so skilled and experienced players can really win here. In Vegas, there are many two and five-dollar blackjack tables, as well as higher ones, as well, such as ten and twenty-dollar blackjack.

The Game

In most casinos, the dealer will deal two cards to each player, and two also to him or herself. If you wish to get a third card, tap the table. If you want to stand, as it is called, wave your hand. If you cards total twenty, for example, and the dealer's cards total eighteen, you win!

As mentioned, in a casino, hand signals are very important. Make sure to always respect the dealer's orders, as a very visible pit boss, (as the dealer's boss, is known), is always loitering nearby, and will make you very uncomfortable if you break a rule. You can easily be asked to leave the game if you don't follow the very specific rules of blackjack. The "eyes in the sky", as the notorious Las Vegas security is known, is always watching you, so be careful. If you have 21, you of course, win blackjack automatically.

Blackjack is a fun game to play with old friends or new friends. Yes, it can be a little intimidating to play with strangers, but it really is a good way to bond with fellow travelers who, like you may never played this game before. It's a good idea, as well, to learn some strategy before you head to the tables, or even take a class, as we mentioned, as you will likely enjoy the experience more when you know more about the game.

In blackjack, face cards – the queen, king, and jack, are all worth ten, while an ace can either be an 11 or a 1.

Hot tip! Never touch your cards, or anyone else's cards, in a casino table game. You will quickly get a verbal reprimand. Also – make sure to not blow smoke in anyone's face while at a table game or a slot machine. We always try to observe these etiquette rules at all times.

There are also many v   ckjack games in most casinos, which we prefer, because they are a little less intimida ng then sidling up to a table, especially one with other guests.

Player Options

- **Stand** – The player does not take any more cards.
- **Hit** – The player will take one more card.
- **Double down** – The player is allowed to take one more card with the promise that they will then stand.
- **Split** - If the player's first two cards have the same exact value, then the player is allowed to split them into two separate hands. The player can then play these two hands.

Player Tips

- It is always wise to stand when you have a combined total of 17.
- It is also wise to hit when you are below 17.
- Try the following websites to really learn more about blackjack: **www.wikipedia.com, bettingexpert.com, www.blackjackage.com, and www.freeblackjackdoc.com.**

Craps

One of the lesser-known casino games, craps is a complicated game that is best learned by a lot of practice and patience. The purpose is to make wagers on the outcome of rolling a pair of dice. Each player takes turns rolling a pair of dice, and each player makes wagers on what the dice will read after rolled. For example, if I am playing, I can wager that the number on the pair of dice will equal a 10. Players can also wager against each other and/or the dealer. The player rolling the dice is called the "shooter".

Sound confusing? It is a bit, but practice makes improvement, as we like to say! It may be a good idea to simply watch a few games of craps as you wander the casinos.

Poker

Poker is a game usually played by experienced players, and it takes practice to really learn it. This is actually the most popular card game in the world, and was invented in Germany, way back in the 1500's. It is extremely big in Vegas, and there are many poker tournaments in Sin City each year. Many professional poker players make their home in Vegas, making a great living doing what they love.

The premise of poker is to end up with a great hand of five cards. Specifically, players want five of a kind – five of the same card, such as a ten, and also pairs of cards, such as two kings or two queens. A straight flush is the king of all hands, and this is a very rare collection of the following cards: king, queen, ace, ten, and jack.

Betting and bluffing are two key elements of poker, and the phrase "poker face" is notorious with this game. Players love to bet and bluff their way to victory. A good website is **www.bicyclecards.com,** and it will help you better understand this fun and addictive game.

Roulette

A giant wheel is what we think of when we hear the word "roulette", which actually means "little wheel" in French. The game of Roulette comes from France, and has become very popular throughout the world. A giant, gleaming wheel of alternating red and black spaces with numbers is the centerpiece for this casino game. You can bet on red or black, and also add a number to your bet, if you wish. Players can also bet on odd or even numbers, so you have a lot of choices here to pick from. The "croupier", as the dealer is known, spins the wheel after all players have made their bets. Roulette is a fun and non-stressful game to start your casino journey with.

Slots

Very quickly, visitors to Las Vegas will be amazed by the sheer volume and variety of slot machines in this city. From the minute you step off your plane, the first thing you will see is a row of slot machines, all lined up, just waiting to be used!

Fun, zany themes abound in each casino that decorate the thousands and thousands of slot machines in this city. New movies and old movies, as well as images of celebrities are on display on these highly addictive machines. It is not uncommon to see a giant superhero-themed slot machine, or Britney Spears or another celebrity on one.

The limits on a slot machine range from a penny to a hundred dollars. The more lines you play, which also equals paying more, is directly correlated to the higher your payout can be. For example, if you sit down at a 25-cent machine, and play only one line, or 25 cents, your payout will be much less (if you win), than if you bet 75 cents each time you play.

Casinos to Explore

When you visit Vegas, a must-do is to explore the many casinos as you wander this city. Each is unique, of course, and here are some of the better ones. As a basic rule, the larger casinos are found on the Strip, and the smaller, cozier ones can be found off-Strip, particularly in the downtown area. It's fun to explore both to simply see that is more your style. Each one is unique and special.

Bellagio

www.bellagio.com. 1.702.693.7111. 3600 Las Vegas Blvd. South.

Elegant but not stuffy, Bellagio's expansive, inviting casino is decked out in shades of maroon and yellow. Right off the beautiful lobby, the casino snakes its way around this resort, and the table games tend to be expensive, but, rest assured, there are many, many affordable slot machines.

Adjacent to the casino is the famous indoor conservatory, with its whimsical themes that change each few weeks. Wander through the conservatory and then head straight to the casino. The theme in the casino is upscale Italian elegance, which suits us just fine!

Monte Carlo

www.montecarlolasvegas.com. 1.702.730.7777. 3700 Las Vegas Blvd. South.

Maybe it's just us, but the smell in this casino is magical. Is it vanilla? We're not sure, but every time we smell this particular scent when we are back home, we think of the immaculately clean and chic casino at Monte Carlo. This was the first Vegas casino that we ever stepped foot in, so we hold a special spot in our hearts for the Monte Carlo.

Unlike a lot of many Vegas casinos, which are spread out and can be downright confusing, the casino here is a giant rectangle, and visitors can easily master the layout quickly. The lighting is bright and elegant, and you feel like you are in a classy place.

Paris

www.parislasvegas.com. 1.702.946.7000. 3655 Las Vegas Blvd. South

Bonjour! Welcome to the City of Light! Yes, this is not the real Paris, but it does feel oddly similar to the real City of Lights. If you've ever been to the real Paris, the beige look of the buildings, interspersed with plenty of colorful cafes and storefronts is also what you will get at

Paris Las Vegas. The theme here is wonderfully executed, and we may be biased, but we have always done well in the casino here, which makes us love it even more!

The feeling here as you wander of play some slots or a table game is of upscale elegance, but never snobbery. There is a very nice variety of slot and table games here, to suit anyone's vacation budget. Bonne chance! (good luck).

Venetian

www.venetian.com. 1.866.659.9643. 3355 Las Vegas Blvd. South.

Much like the actual Venice, the casino and entire Venetian hotel is immaculate and makes you truly feel like you are in the city of Venice. The casino here is both expansive and attractive, with a wide variety of both games and slots. Limits tend to be higher here, because the property is five-star, but rest assured, there are still plenty of real-people games, such as quarter slot machines and five and ten-dollar blackjack tables.

All around the casino are nice spots for dining and shopping, as the Grand Canal Shoppes are located right upstairs. A bevy of dining options are also conveniently located, and include a nice food court adjacent to the casino.

Wynn

www.wynnlasvegas.com. 1.702.770.7100. 3799 Las Vegas Blvd. South.

The casino at Wynn is very similar to Bellagio's opulent casino. There really is no theme here, but this casino is plain beautiful, filled with fresh, colorful flowers everywhere you look. As you enter, a flowered merry-go-round (just for show), greets guests, setting the scene for this magnificent, airy casino.

Beautiful, upscale shops and cafes abound in the Wynn, and be sure to check out the very pricey but sumptuous buffet. The Wynn is a special place, and the bright, fun casino also offers a wide variety of games to indulge in.

Off-Strip

Many off-Strip casinos are known as locals' casinos – that is, they appeal mostly to locals. Casinos like Texas Station and many downtown casinos are locals casinos, and many Vegas residents routinely visit their favorite casino.

Why do many Vegas residents prefer off-Strip casinos? Because these hotels are usually way less expensive overall than the big, flashy Strip hotels, meaning that they offer lower limits on blackjack and other games. These locals casinos are also way more inexpensive when it comes to dining options, as well, which allows them to dine and play the slots more.

Four Queens

www.fourqueens.com. 1.702.385.4011. 202 Fremont Street, Las Vegas.

A beautiful, old-fashioned casino with a lot of charm, the casino at Four Queens is pretty small. An ornate, huge glass chandelier covers a big portion of the gaming floor. A small food court and several nice restaurants, like Hugo's Cellar, pepper this casino. It is a nice place to simply wander and play some slots or a game of blackjack with friendly, affable dealers.

A huge variety of slots and table games are available, and you can find many very inexpensive games, such as $2 - dollar blackjack and many penny slots. You will not break your budget in the Four Queens casino, that is for sure!

Golden Nugget

www.goldennugget.com. 1.702.385.7111. 129 East Fremont Street, Las Vegas.

When you see this large casino, your first thought may be "Hey, this seems like a casino on the Strip". The Golden Nugget was founded by Steve Wynn, who is really the father of Las Vegas hotels. This casino, as we stated, feels like it could belong right on the Strip.

The casino signs and layout just feel very Strip-like, and there is a plethora of shops and restaurants that surround this airy, bright casino. There is a nice variety of both table games and slot machines to satisfy anyone's budget, and we enjoy simply taking an hour or two to really explore this gem of a casino.

Main Street Station

This smaller casino is pleasant to explore, and has some nice dining options that abound. It feels older, and it is – Main Street Station is very historic, and many touches invoke early San Francisco. Stained glass and ornate chandeliers will let you know that you are in a smaller, cozier than the ones found on the Strip.

Main Street is connected to the California resort, and it's also a nice, safe two-minute walk to the Plaza and other Fremont Street hotels. We have always enjoyed the people and the feel of this small resort. Many table and slots are cheaper here than in most resorts, making this a relaxed place to play.

Chapter 8

Thrills & Adrenaline – Las Vegas

Las Vegas is not just about the casinos, shopping malls, and great dining. In the last ten years, Vegas has also built quite a reputation nationwide for its extreme sports – gun ranges, extreme driving ranges, and car racing. Vegas truly has fun activities for everyone, whether you are into shopping, hiking, guns, or really, really fast cars! Many of these activities and excursions come with a large fee, but hiking is one of the cheap alternatives to these, and it's also great exercise.

Your best bets for adrenaline junkies are detailed below. Have fun, and make sure to buckle up!

Fun tip! Make sure to look into the Thrills Pass, which can be booked on www.tripadvisor.com or through www.vegas.com. The number for www.vegas.com is: 1.866.983.4279. This pass allows you to visit four thrills attractions over a 2-day period, and can save you a good bit of money. Attractions include the four thrill rides at the Stratosphere and also the VooDoo zipline at the Fremont Street experience.

New York New York's Big Apple Coaster

www.newyorknewyork.com. 1.702.740.6969. Cost: $14. Hours: Sun-Thur, 11 am – 11 pm. Fri & Sat, 10:30 am – 12 am.

Roller coaster lovers, check this one out! You can see the Big Apple Coaster as you walk along the Strip, as it dips and dives right around the perfect reproduction known as New York, New York resort and casino. This coaster travels at a top speed of 67 mph, and its' biggest dip is a whopping 144 feet.

This coaster is not exactly a smooth ride, and there are several inversions, so be prepared, and make sure you have a strong stomach for this one!

Richard Petty Driving Experience

www.drivepetty.com. 1.800.237.3889. 7000 North Las Vegas Blvd. Cost: $109 - $135 for a ride-along & $109 - $159 for a Race Ride. Hours: Most days, 11 am & 1:30 pm.

If you love Nascar and want to experience the feel of a true Nascar experience, this is the attraction for you. Here, at the Las Vegas Motor Speedway, about 15 miles from the heart of the Strip, you can either ride 3 laps with a professional driver or have a solo ride that will cost you a bit more.

Of course, a valid drivers' license is required, and there are weight limits, as well. The staff is attentive and gracious, and we feel this is a great value – this is bucket list stuff, so check this one out.

Slotzilla Zipline – Fremont Experience

www.vegasexperience.com. 1.844.947.8342. Cost: $20 for upper zipline & $40 for lower zipline. Hours: Sun – Thur, 1 pm - 1 am & Fri. & Sat, 1 pm – 2 am.

Have you ever wanted to fly across a crowded street? Well, you're in luck, because in Las Vegas, anything goes! Similar to the VooDoo zipline at the Rio, detailed below, the Slotzilla Zipline is a thrilling experience high above Fremont Street.

The Zipline thrusts several riders at a time out of a giant replica of a slot machine – you have to see this one in person to really believe it! Riders fly, face-down, almost like a superhero, from one of two ziplines – either an upper one, at a height of 114 feet, or a lower one, at a height of 77 feet. Either ride you take is a fun and unique experience. Please note, however, that this attraction does have weight and height restrictions.

Stratosphere Thrill Rides

www.stratospherehotel.com. 1.702.380.7777. 2000 Las Vegas Blvd. South. Cost: Observation deck with 1 ride: $20, with 2 rides: $25, with 3 rides: $35 / Unlimited observation deck with the BigShot, X-Scream and Insanity rides: $39.95. Skyjump: $119.99. Hours: Sun – Thur, 10 am – 1 am. Fri & Sat, 10 am – 2 am.

The amazing observation deck at the top of the Stratosphere Hotel stands at over 900 feet tall, and is an attraction in itself. Four other death-defying attractions are also housed here, at the top of this hotel.

*__Skyjump__ - Jump off the base of the hotel, from a height of 829 feet. This jump holds the Guinness Record for the world's highest controlled descent, and costs $119.99. Clearly, the Skyjump is only for the most daring of us all!

*__BigShot__ – Fly 160 feet into the air at 45 miles per hour, and then descend back to Earth on this ride.

*__X-Scream__ – Dangle 27 feet over the edge of the hotel in this roller-coaster style ride, 866 feet over the Earth.

*__Insanity__ - Yes, the name aptly describes this very well! Insanity takes riders in a face-down drop from your starting point of 900 feet above the ground. The force here equals 3G's, so you may want to watch this one before you try it!

Las Vegas Exotics Rentals

www.vegasexoticsrentals.com. **1.866.871.1893. 5115 Dean Martin Drive, Las Vegas.**
Cost: varies.

Have you ever seen a car and thought to yourself "I would love to drive that!"? Well, you can at Vegas Exotic Rentals, a very hip place that rents out every conceivable kind of luxury car you can imagine. Our personal favorite is the Lamborghini, pictured above. This is the kind of place that dreams come true!

The legendary Italian car, the Lamborghini Gallardo Spyder, can be rented for a mere $575 for 6 hours or 24 hours for $775. A security deposit is required for the more expensive models. Guests can also rent a bevy of cars like Bentleys, BMWS, Mercedes, Lotuses, and Aston Martins. This is a fun spot for the thrill seekers in your party, or just to feel a bit richer for a few hours.

Vegas Indoor Skydiving

www.vegasindoorskydiving.com. 1.702.731.4768. 200 Convention Center Drive, Las Vegas. Cost: $75 for 3 minutes. Hours: Daily, 9:45 am – 8 pm.

If you have ever wanted to experience a true sensation of skydiving, Las Vegas Indoor Skydiving is the place for you. Prices are steep, at $75 for only three minutes of fun, but this is a very unique attraction. Located right near the Convention Center, just off the Strip, it is a quick taxi ride or stop on the monorail.

Prices include special training, and please be aware that there are specific weight limits that are correlated to height, as only the most aerodynamic flyers are allowed to experience this attraction. Indoor skydiving is very popular with younger guests, and this place is very busy, so plan accordingly.

VooDoo Zipline – Rio Las Vegas

www.riolasvegas.com. 1.702.388.0477. 3700 West Flamingo Rd, Las Vegas. Cost: $27.49. Hours: Daily, 11 am – 11 pm.

Adjacent to the very cool VooDoo nightclub and lounge, atop the similarly cool Rio Las Vegas resort, the VooDoo zipline is a thrilling attraction that packs quite a punch.

The zipline whisks daring souls from the hotel's Masquerade tower, 800 feet to its' Ipanema tower. Then, it whisks you back 800 feet backwards, which is quite a sensation in itself. The zipline travels up to 33 mph, and it's a very cool experience to look down at the twinkling lights of Vegas, if you do experience this attraction at night.

Wet 'n Wild Las Vegas

www.wetnwildlasvegas.com. 1.702.830.7975. 7055 South Fort Appache Rd, Las Vegas, 89148. Cost: $64.99+ for season tickets / $29.99: kids, single day tickets & $39.99: adults, single day tickets. Hours: Varies, but most days 10:30 am - 6 pm.

The well-known Wet 'n Wild water parks that are popular throughout the country now have a park in Las Vegas – in the middle of the desert! On a hot day, this park can be brutal in terms of the lack of shade, but the water slides and lazy rivers make it all worth it, in our opinion.

This is also a very affordable day, as you note the moderate prices for such a famous and well-rounded water park. Several thrilling slides such as the Canyon Cliffs, the Constrictor, and the Rattler are for the most daring of your party. An expansive wave pool and a huge, 1,100-foot lazy river add to the fun of this park. Kids' rides such as the Desert Racers, which has multiple lanes for kids and adults to race against each other, on a gentle hill, are also fun.

Wet 'n Wild also features five eateries, including the Oasis Café, which serves regular and healthy fare, as well as one retail shop. Check out this park, if you have time – it is very nicely done and a fun time for singles and the entire family. There is truly something for everyone at this park.

Chapter 9- Attractions for All Ages

Las Vegas offers many educational and fun activities that will actually appeal to many different ages. We've weeded through the many that this city has to offer and listed only the ones that we find may be the most enjoyable for your party.

Bellagio Gallery of Fine Arts

www.bellagio.com. 1.702.693.7111. 3600 Las Vegas Blvd. South. Cost: $18. Hours: Daily, 10 am – 8 pm.

The Bellagio Gallery of Fine Arts is a small gallery that packs quite a big punch. Past exhibits have included Diego, Renoir, Picasso, Warhol, and Faberge, and there is almost always a major exhibit going on here. Suitable for all ages, this gallery appeals most to (of course) art-lovers, and is a very fun way to spend a few hours.

The gallery itself is very small, with only two rooms, and there is also a nicely stocked gift shop to peruse after you enjoy the works of art by major artists. This gallery can also be a nice way to escape the craziness of Vegas! We would allot at least an hour or two to really peruse the works here.

The Eiffel Tower Experience

www.parislasvegas.com. 1.702.946.7000. 3655 Las Vegas Blvd. South. Cost: $14.25: day admission / $19.25: night admission. Hours: Mon – Fri, 9:30 am – 12:30 am / Sat & Sun, 9:30 am – 1:00 am.

A very popular attraction in Las Vegas, the Eiffel Tower Attraction is a must-see for the Paris lover in your party. OK, so this one-half scale replica doesn't exactly stack up to the real Eiffel

Tower, but it's still impressive, standing at a whopping 541 feet. A very knowledgeable guide will whisk you and other visitors up the elevator to the top of the tower, where the whole city seems to stretch in front of you.

We do recommend partaking in this attraction at night, when the city positively lights up. One really cool thing here, too, is that the fountains of Bellagio are right across the street, so your view at night will definitely be worth the price of admission. The sight of these dancing fountains is one of the most unique experiences in this city.

Gondola Rides – The Venetian

www.venetian.com. 1.702.414.4300. 3355 Las Vegas Blvd. South. Cost: $34/person for shared gondola. $136 for private gondola. Hours: Sun-Thur, 10 am – 11 pm / Friday & Saturday, 10 am – 12 am.

Venice, anyone? The world-famous gondola rides in Venice, Italy are recreated here, at the Venetian. We've heard that many real Italian gondola rides are often not worth the money, as the gondoliers will shorten your trip significantly.

Here, however, at the five-star Venetian, rest assured, you will get your money's worth. You can choose to reserve an outside ride through the canals that afford a great view of the Strip, or an indoor ride through the Grand Canal Shoppes. Also, a shared gondola is a heck of a lot cheaper than a private one, but the privacy is very nice, we must admit. Several of the gondoliers will sing to you, and a few are natives of Italy, which is a cool bonus. This is a fun and very kitschy activity, but for many, it is a Las Vegas must.

High Roller – Linq

www.caesars.com. 1.702.322.0593. 3545 Las Vegas Blvd. South. Cost: $19.98 for regular car, $35.49 for open bar car. Hours: Most days, 12 pm – 12 am.

A fairly new attraction to the always-burgeoning Las Vegas scene, the High Roller can also be found in many other American and international cities, like Paris and Orlando. This one, located in the Linq outdoor shopping promenade, has become a very popular attraction in Sin City.

It is the tallest observation wheel in the world, and also a whopping 520 feet in diameter. The High Roller takes 30 minutes to completely revolve, and you may have to share your cabin with another family, so keep this little nugget of information handy!

An open-bar cabin is also available for guests over the age of 21, and this is a popular girls and gals' night out option in Vegas. The views here, of the city and the mountains, are an added bonus.

The Lion Ranch

www.lionhabitatranch.org. 1.702.595.6666. 382 Bruner Ave. Henderson, NV. Cost: $24.99. Hours: Fri – Mon, 10 am – 2 pm.

If you are familiar with Las Vegas from five or so years ago, you will know that the MGM Grand used to host a very cool attraction. The Lion exhibit showcased a variety of very cute lions that would roam in a giant glass enclosure that was situated smack dab in the center of the casino. A few years back, this exhibit was moved to a more permanent site in nearby Henderson, and it is a joy to visit these giant creatures. Yes, we miss being able to see these amazing creatures anytime we used to stroll through the MGM, but at least they are still around, and are still thriving.

This is a fairly small zoo, and admission is $24.99 and includes the lion exhibits. Guests can also interact with a few giraffes and a few species of birds, as well. Ozzie the giraffe will show you his painting skills, and guests can also feed this gentle giant. The Lion Ranch exhibit features several lions of all ages, and is very educational for kids and adults alike. Children get free admission on the month they were born, which, we think, is a pretty nice perk!

The Mob Museum

www.mobmuseum.org. 1.702.229.2734. 300 Stewart Ave, Las Vegas. Cost: $21.98. Hours: Daily, 9 am – 9pm.

The Godfather, anyone?

OK, so this one might be a little more for adults, but it's still an educational experience for all ages. You can spend a few hours teaching your children why *not* to be a mob boss after visiting this fun and interactive museum. Located in downtown Las Vegas, this museum offers three floors of artifacts and exhibits detailing why and how both the American mob and the Las Vegas mob affected the people and culture of America.

For movie fans, there is even a whole wall dedicated to the many mob movies that have been produced, many of them very successfully, in America. This museum is very unique, and will help you see the mob in a whole new light by the end of your tour here.

The Nevada State Museum & Historical Society and the Springs Preserve

www.nevadastatemuseum.com. 1.702.486.5205. 309 South Valley View, Las Vegas. Cost: $17.98. Hours: Daily, 9 am – 5 pm.

Attention, history lovers in your party – visit this place! One of your fellow authors holds a degree in History, so the Nevada State Museum was right up his alley! Adjacent to this museum stands the Springs Preserve, which is a very pleasant stretch of the Mojave Desert, with many fascinating wildlife exhibits. In order to explore the Springs Preserve, you pay one ticket which also includes admission to the museum.

The state museum is a very informative museum explaining in detail, and with many exhibits about the history of the Silver State, as Nevada is known. Fossils of the many animals who roam the surrounding desert are also on full display here. A fully-stocked gift shop sells all sorts of souvenirs and trinkets. Outside is a bonus - the museum has amazing views of the Strip and the city of Las Vegas.

Chapter 10 – Kid-Friendly Attractions

Despite the "Sin City" name, Las Vegas is, in reality, pretty kid-friendly, and if you look closely, you will see this during your visit to Vegas. From mini-golf to food courts to theme parks, this town has it all. Even the sheer number of bakeries and ice cream shops help make Vegas a haven for children of all ages.

Adventuredome – Circus Circus

www.adventuredome.com. 1.702.734.0410. 2880 Las Vegas Blvd. South. Price: Moderate / Adults: $31.95 for all-day pass & Kids: $17.95 for all-day pass. Cost - Individual rides: $6 - $12. Hours: Most days: 10 am – 12 am. Some days until 9 pm; varies.

Kids will love this place, that's for sure! The world's largest indoor amusement park, the Adventuredome features a fun, affordable day for the whole family. This nicely decorated, safe, and clean theme park features a ride-by-ride payment plan and also all-day passes, which are very popular and your best bet.

Even if you are not staying at Circus Circus, you will want to make the pilgrimage here to experience the world's largest indoor theme park. Kids and adults alike will likely enjoy this place, especially if you are an adrenaline junkie.

The Adventuredome features several stomach churning rides, like the ride aptly named Chaos, and two daring roller coasters. El Loco is the only indoor, double-roll, double-loop rollercoaster in the world. There are also many kid-friendly, tamer rides, as well as family rides, as well like bumper cards. This is a great place to spend a few hours, and be sure to check out the cute souvenir shops right outside this theme park.

Discovery Children's Museum

www.discoverychildrensmuseum.com. 1.702.382.5437. 360 Promenade Place, Las Vegas. Cost: Moderate / Adults & Children over age one: $14.95, under one: free. Hours: Tues – Fri, 9 am – 4 pm. Sat, 10 am – 5 pm, Sun, 12 pm – 5 pm.

A wonderful interactive museum, Discovery Children's Museum will take your child through 9 major interactive scientific exhibits. You and your kids can wander the carefully chosen exhibit, and, in many cases, actually interact with each.

Current exhibits include a section called "Patent Pending", which teaches kids about inventions, and also "Waterworld", allowing kids to learn about the Earth's water supply and our five oceans. Over 1 million visitors have come here since its' inception, and this museum is a nice respite from the often chaotic Las Vegas scene.

A wonderful gift store is also on the premises, and all goods are tax-free. Scores of games, books, and, of course – stuffed animals, are the big draws here.

Fun Dungeon & Fantasy Faire – Excalibur

www.excalibur.com. 1.702.597.7700. 3850 Las Vegas Blvd. South. Cost: $2+ per game. Hours: Daily, 10 am – 10 pm.

Excalibur is a really well-themed Medieval resort located on the southern end of the Strip, and its' Fun Dungeon and Fantasy Faire is truly a kids' paradise. These attractions are located right underneath the casino, at the far end of this massive resort.

As soon as you enter this resort from the Strip entrance, take the stairs down and you will be immediately engulfed in a large and noisy arcade. Much like your typical arcade, the Fun Dungeon features typical fair-style games that you pay for individually, and also video games, as well.

Make sure to really explore the Excalibur resort after you spend some time here, as this entire resort, with its' fun food court and medieval-themed shops, is all very kid-pleasing.

Hershey's Chocolate World

www.hersheyschocolateworld.lasvegas.com. 1.702.740.6969. 3790 Las Vegas Blvd. South. (in New York, New York). Free admission. Hours: Daily, 9 am – 11 pm.

A bastion of kid-friendliness, Hershey's Chocolate World is a huge retail store and bakery dedicated to - you guessed it, Hershey's candies. Yes, one of America's best-loved candy companies has set up shop in New York, New York, right next to the casino. Open from 9 am to 11 pm, this store features an interactive experience where you can actually film an ad for Reese's peanut butter cups, and you can also customize and buy your own chocolate bar.

A giant bakery with all sorts of baked goods featuring Hershey's chocolates is here, as well, and they sell amazing coffee specialty drinks, as well. Of course, the giant retail shop is fully-stocked with all sorts of candy, apparel, and stuffed animals.

Kiss Monster Mini Golf – Rio Resort and Casino

www.kissmonsterminigolf.com. 1.702.558.6256. 3700 West Flamingo Rd. Cost: $11.98 for all. Hours: Daily, 10 am – midnight.

Located at the Rio resort and casino, just west of the Strip, Kiss Monster Mini Golf can be a unique way to spend a few hours. Clearly, the name itself can tell you that the theme here is the Kiss rock group, with their over-the-top style and music.

Kiss Monster Mini Golf is actually housed inside the Rio Resort's Masquerade shopping village, and is a glow-in-the-dark 18-hole mini-golf course. There is also a giant arcade to occupy the kids, as well as a DJ that spins tunes, a huge gift shop, and yes, even a Kiss-themed wedding chapel here. Needless to say, this is not exactly like your putt-putt place back home!

M & M's World – Showcase Mall

www.mmsworld.com. 1.800.651.2437. 3785 Las Vegas Blvd. South. (next to MGM Grand, inside the Showcase Mall.) Free admission. Hours: Daily, 9 am – 12 am.

A haven to any kid, really, the M & M's World receives very high reviews from guests, and is a true winner. Guests can explore a 4-story haven of this tasty chocolate treat, and also experience a fun 4D movie, as well. Make sure to customize your assortment of M & M's candies, and shop till you drop at this huge retail space.

Open daily from 9 am to 12 am, this retail and interactive space is located inside the Showcase Mall, right next to the Coca-Cola store. It is truly a fun way to spend a few hours, and to shop for some cool memorabilia, such as M & M's collectibles, unique candy dispensers and a wide variety of apparel for kids and adults.

Madam Tussaud's Wax Museum – Venetian

www.maddamtussauds.com.las-vegas. 1.866.841.3739. 3377 Las Vegas Blvd. South, Suite 2001. Price from $26.99. Hours: Mon – Thur & Sun, 10 am – 8 pm. Fri & Sat, 10 am – 9 pm.

Like the other Madam Tussaud's worldwide, this location at the Venetian is a haven for lovers of celebrities. Numerous famous actors, actresses, musicians, and sports stars have been meticulously reproduced by very talented artists. The funny thing is that celebrities are usually smaller than people think they are, so it's amusing to see how much smaller these celebs really are.

With locations around the world, including in New York City, Madam Tussaud's has a great reputation for their stunning works. New celebrity replicas are created all the time, and it's simply a fun sight to see recreations of stars like Brad Pitt, Sandra Bullock, and Britney Spears. Even superheroes like Spiderman and the Hulk are perfectly recreated and on display here. Please note that no food or drinks are allowed here, and there is no café onsite, but the Venetian and many other resorts are a short stroll away.

Marvel Avengers S.T.A.T.I.O.N.

www.stationattraction.com. 1.702.894.7626. Cost: $34: adults / $24: kids, ages 4-11. Hours: Daily, 10 am – 10 pm.

Located inside Treasure Island, this new attraction on the Strip will appeal to the sci/fi geek in your family! You will get a chance to explore many of the Marvel characters and their gadgets. From Thor to Captain America, visitors travel through a series of very interactive exhibits, answering questions as they go, so a vast knowledge of Marvel characters will be very helpful here!

The more you know, the better and quicker you can move through this fast-paced attraction. Reviews on this attraction are mixed, but many hard-core fans will enjoy this very interactive attraction. As expected, a fully-stocked gift shop is here, as well, offering lots of fun merchandise.

New York, New York's Roller Coaster & Arcade

www.newyorknewyork.com. 1.702.740.6969. 3790 Las Vegas Blvd. South. Cost: $14. Hours: Sunday – Thursday, 11 am – 11 pm. Friday & Saturday, 10:30 am - 12 am.

As you can see from this very steep hill, the New York, New York roller coaster is definitely not for the faint of heart! This coaster makes several huge drops, the steepest one being 144 feet, so it will for sure appeal to thrill seekers. It travels at 67 mph, as well, and has great views of the Strip, if you can tear yourself away from the thrill of the ride itself.

We have heard reports, and actually experienced it ourselves, that this is not the smoothest coaster, so be aware of this before deciding to ride this coaster.

Conveniently located inside New York, New York, this is fun thrill with great views of the Strip. A nice but small arcade is located inside, as you approach the line for this roller coaster.

Siegfried & Roy's Secret Garden and Dolphin Habitat – The Mirage

www.mirage.com. 1.702.791.7111. 3400 Las Vegas Blvd. South. Cost: $22: adults / $17: kids. Hours: Monday – Friday, 11 am – 6:30 pm. Saturday & Sunday, 10 am – 6:30 pm.

A thrill for many visitors, this immersive habitat operated by the Mirage is the brain child of famed and now retired illusionists Siegfried and Roy. These magicians enjoyed a storied career with their show at the Mirage until a tragic accident over ten years ago ended their show. Shortly after, they opened this fun exhibit that included two areas – a secret garden where guests can view tigers and lions, and also a dolphin exhibit. Do these employees have the best jobs in Vegas, or what?

Set in the tropical oasis of the Mirage, this experience is located just outside the casino's shopping arcade and adjacent to the lush pool area. Many guests prefer the dolphin experience, where you can ogle and play with these playful creatures. If you pay less and skip the dolphin experience, rest assured, you will still have a great time experiencing these exotic and beautiful white tigers and lions. The staff members are gracious and helpful, and really seem to enjoy their jobs.

Red Rock National Conservation Area

www.redrockcanyonlv.org. 1.702.515.5379. 1000 Scenic Loop Drive, Las Vegas. Cost: $3 : pedestrian, motorcycle & $7: cars. Hours: Daily, 9 am – 5 pm.

Currently, Red Rock is the number one attraction in Las Vegas on www.tripadvisor.com, proving that this is a very well-respected attraction in Vegas. A true touch of nature, Red Rock makes you feel very quickly like you are in the middle of a desert, which, coincidentally - you are! The nature enthusiasts in your party will love this stunning national conservation area. Nevada is truly a beautiful state, with towering mountains and dry heat.

Hiking trails and horseback riding are the big draws at Red Rock, and they only charge a nominal fee for cars and other vehicles that park here. The well-stocked visitors center, which includes a nice book and gift store, is open daily from 8 am until 4:30 pm.

You can also buy an annual pass for $30, which can be a good value if you are here a lot, as many locals are. Make sure to wear sunscreen and really good hiking shoes or sneakers.

Shark Reef – Mandalay Bay

www.manadalaybay.com. 1.702.632.7777. 3950 Las Vegas Blvd. South. Cost: $20 adults / $14 kids. Hours: Sun – Thur, 10 am – 8 pm & Fri. and Sat, 10 am – 10 pm.

Have you heard that simply being around animals can lower your blood pressure? Well, then its' actually healthy to visit this fun, smaller aquarium in Mandalay Bay. Located in a way off part of Mandalay Bay, this attraction is certainly worth the walk if you are an animal lover, like we are. An immersive, long tunnel leads guests through millions of gallons of sharks and fish.

A komodo dragon exhibit it also fun for the kids of all ages. An audio tour is available for guests, and you can easily spend a few hours here examining all the amazing animals. Exotic sharks, endangered green sea turtles, stingrays, and jellyfish are just some of the 2,000 creatures you will experience at this educational attraction.

The Shark Reef also offers some pretty cool options for guests of all ages. You can pay an extra fee to feed the stingrays, green sea turtles, and the sharks. For a whopping $650, you can also splurge and actually dive with the sharks, which will definitely raise your blood pressure, we would think!!

Tournament of Kings

www.excalibur.com. 1.702.597.7600. 3850 Las Vegas Blvd South. (in Excalibur). Cost: $73. Hours: Daily, 6 pm and 8:30 pm (most days).

A very popular show that is also extremely kid-friendly, Tournament of Kings is located in the Excalibur hotel. It is a Medieval-themed dinner show and entertainment show, and can get very exciting very quickly.

Actors play medieval jousters who battle each other while galloping at full speed around a very themed indoor theater. Dinner is served as you watch the show, much like the dinner show Medieval Times, which many guests may have experienced back home.

You don't have a choice of what's for dinner – at press time, it is tomato soup, steamed broccoli, a Cornish hen, a biscuit, and an apple puff pastry for dessert. Adults can also order drinks that start at $10 each. Book this one early, as it is a huge crowd-pleaser! Prices are pretty steep, starting at $84.99. Drinks will set you back at least $10 each, so factor these prices into your budget.

Chapter 11 – Entertainment

Nightlife and entertainment in Las Vegas are almost synonymous. Big-name headliners, famous magic acts, and new, exciting names are always coming to town. The entertainment scene is always changing and getting better, and it's an exciting experience for Vegas visitors to catch a show or a concert. The caliber is almost always on par with Broadway shows.

A few years ago, when Phantom of the Opera had a residency at the Venetian, we watched with awe as the understudy for Christine, the main character, was the most amazing Christine that we had ever seen on stage, and we have seen the show on Broadway several times! The show was top-notch, and the set was on par with any Broadway set I've ever seen.

In this chapter, we will detail many of the entertainment options. Like dining and shopping options, Las Vegas truly has something for everyone in this department.

Hot tip! Use the Tix 4 Tonite booth in Las Vegas for your tickets, if you can. There are multiple locations in Vegas, including one at Circus Circus, Four Queens, and one outside the World of Coca-Cola. Discounts can be had for almost every show in Vegas, and most shows will be discounted on most days. This can be a HUGE savings for your trip, if you can find your show (which you usually can), and you attend more than one show during your trip!

Entertainment

Comedy

The comedy scene in Las Vegas is always growing, and you can find many funny people in this town like Nathan Burton and Mac King, who are magicians who we profile later in this chapter. Brad Garrett, the actor/comedian has a very funny show if you enjoy this type of entertainment, and the Aces of Comedy show at the Mirage is also a good bet.

Aces of Comedy - The Mirage

www.mirage.com. 1.702.791.7111. 3400 Las Vegas Blvd. South. Nightly, 10 pm. Tickets from $80.

Set in the Terry Fator theater, a beautiful spot inside the tropical Mirage resort, the Aces of Comedy is a great bet if you are a huge fan of comedy. If laughs are your thing, then this is one of the best bets in town, and affordable, as well.

Big names perform here, including Ray Romano, David Spade, Jay Leno, and Tim Allen. Like Brad Garrett's Comedy Club, listed below, this show also receives many awards for its' lineup of comedians and the truly funny men and women who perform here.

Brad Garrett's Comedy Club – MGM Grand

www.mgmgrand.com. **1.702.891.7777. 3799 Las Vegas Blvd. South. Tickets from $51.99. Nightly, 8 pm.**

Well-known comedian and actor Brad Garrett, widely known from the show "Everybody Loves Raymond", headlines at his own comedy club inside the MGM Grand. This show consistently wins accolades and raves from guests.

Brad Garrett is here often, doing his funny stand-up routine, and when he is not performing, you will see at least two other comedians. He employs both seasoned comedians, as well as up-and-comers. Some are more PG-rated, and some are a bit more on the raunchy side, so be aware that this is very much an adult show.

The theater is not huge, and every seat offers good views of the action. You can purchase drinks, which are pricey at $10 each, and also gourmet popcorn, which is also not cheap. Please note that guests are not allowed to bring in food or drink. Enjoy the comedy!

Jerry Seinfeld – Caesar's Palace

www.caesarspalace.com. 1.866.983.4279. 3570 Las Vegas Blvd. South. Tickets from $100. Nightly, 7:30. Days/months vary.

Beloved by millions worldwide, Jerry Seinfeld is a comic genius, and the star of the most successful comedy sitcom of all time, "Seinfeld", which ran for 9 seasons on NBC. He performs off and on at Caesar's Palace, and this show is very popular, and a must for a hard-core Seinfeld fan.

Seinfeld is still a huge and sought-after comedian, and he performs three days a week, on a rotating basis, at the Colosseum, at Caesar's Palace, bringing his unique, hilarious brand of comedy to the stage. Come have some laughs at a beautiful setting, in this grand theater.

Magic

The always burgeoning magic scene in Las Vegas is as good as it's ever been. Amazing talents like the Mindfreak himself, Criss Angel, and other talented illusionists like Nathan Burton and David Copperfield, have all set up residencies in Sin City. If you love magic, like we do, Vegas will not disappoint you!

*Our Pick : Criss Angel – Mindreak Live! – Luxor

www.luxor.com. 1.702.262.4000. 3600 Las Vegas Blvd. South. Tickets from $59. Nightly, 7 and 9:30 pm on most days (varies).

Criss Angel is the most celebrated magician of the twenty-first century, and a Merlin-winner, which is the highest honor any magician can receive. He is also the recipient of the Magician of the Century award, and a four-time Magician of the Year award. You may have seen other magic shows, but to us, this is by far the best magic show in town. Criss Angel can be loud and a bit in your face, but his illusions, energy, and charisma make this show truly spectacular.

Formerly a Cirque show that was wildly successful, there were still often complaints from guests - they either loved the show or hated it. This polarization may have led this talented magician to revamp his show in May of 2016 to a newly named show, Mindfreak Live, which boasts even more illusions and mind-blowing tricks. It is also the most successful magic show of all time in Las Vegas, based on ticket sales.

Over 20 illusions are contained in every show, so the magic geek in your family will most likely enjoy this production! Criss Angel's signature act, levitation, is showcased in Mindfreak Live, and blows most guests' socks off!

The newly vamped show began with standing ovations in each show, so be prepared to be amazed. Tickets begin at around $59 per person, which is a steal for a magician of Angel's caliber and awards. A well-stocked gift shop right outside the theater, as well as several of the magician's custom-made motorcycles are on display, and fun to see.

*David Copperfield – MGM Grand

www.mgmgrand.com. 1.702.891.7777. 3799 Las Vegas Blvd. South. Tickets from $99. Nightly, 7 and 9:30 pm most days (varies).

Another Merlin winner, David Copperfield is famous the world over, and offers a classic magic show at the MGM Grand. If you are seeking a traditional magic show with grand illusions that will make you scratch your head in wonder, this may be the show for you. Personally, this is not our favorite show, and we have seen it twice, but many people love it.

Set in a sumptuous theater at the MGM Grand, Copperfield is a good bet for those new to magic. Copperfield is a great showman, but we feel that a show like Criss Angel has more diversity to it. However, this show will give you a great introduction to an exciting Vegas magic show.

Gregory Popovich's Comedy Pet Theater – Aladdin Theater, Planet Hollywood

www.planethollywoodresort.com. 1.702.785.5555. 3667 Las Vegas Blvd. South. Tickets from $29.95. Daily: 4 pm. Dark: Mondays and Tuesdays.

A kid-friendly magic show in the heart of the Strip, Gregory Popovich is a funny magic and comedy show. Much like Nathan Burton's production, this show is humorous and also features many animals. Starting at $29.95 per ticket, this show is also extremely affordable. Kids and adults alike love this show, and it consistently receives high marks from guests of all ages.

Like Mac King, who also gears his show for the younger set, Popovich utilizes a lot of audience participation, and specifically kids. He is truly a humorous and talented magician.

Mac King Comedy Magic Show – Harrah's

www.caesars.com. 1.702.693.6143. 3475 Las Vegas Blvd. South. Cost: $42.99. Often free with purchase of 2 drinks @ $10 each. Daily: 1 and 3 pm. Dark: Sunday and Monday.

Like Gregory Popovich, Mac King is a great, kid-friendly performer. King has won many awards, and is legendary in the Las Vegas magic scene. King performs mostly smaller illusions in his show, and often pulls eager, happy kids onto stage to help him with his tricks. This show consistently scores very well with audiences, and the kids love it. King is a very funny guy that also incorporates a lot of funny, G-rated humor into his show.

The show often hands out free coupons for this entertaining show. The catch? You do have to buy two drinks, which are $10 each, so for $20, this show is a true steal, and one of the best bargains in all of Las Vegas. One note, however – if you are seeking a magic show with beautiful show girls and huge illusions (aka Criss Angel), do not choose this show! It is very low-key and family friendly.

*Mat Franco – Magic Reinvented Lightly – Linq

www.caesars.com. **1.800.634.6441. 3535 Las Vegas Blvd. South. Tickets from $39. Daily, 4 and 7 pm. Dark: Sundays and Wednesdays.**

A new face in the Vegas magic scene, Mat Franco is the 2014 winner of the very popular show, America's Got Talent. Franco is talented at grand illusions, but focuses more on card tricks and sleight of hand magic, which he performs perfectly. Recently, the relatively young and very charismatic Franco won an award for best magic show in town from the Las Vegas Journal, the city's main newspaper, and we can certainly see why.

Our verdict? Well, your faithful authors are obsessed with magic, and if you like magic, you will probably love this show. Franco carries the show with a great personality combined with amazing tricks and sleight of hand. Check out his show nightly at the Linq, located in the heart of the Strip.

*Top Pick - Nathan Burton – Planet Hollywood

www.planethollywoodresort.com. 1.702.785.5555. 3667 Las Vegas Blvd. South. Tickets from $17. Daily: 4 pm. Dark: Mondays.

Nathan Burton is another former contestant on America's Got Talent, and he is a funny and talented illusionist. Much like Mat Franco, Burton is young and has a great sense of humor. He incorporates his family into his show – his wife is one of the showgirls in the production, and his mother and sister help produce the show.

Burton mixed grand illusions, humor, and great sleight-of-hand in his show, making it a pleasing afternoon, especially for kids, who he often pulls onto the stage to assist him. This is a very kid-friendly show, but also mixes in those big production numbers that will amaze you. Prices start at around $25, so this show is a steal.

*Penn and Teller – Rio

www.pennandteller.com. 1.702.777.7777. 3700 West Flamingo Rd. Tickets from $69. Nightly, 9 pm. Dark: Thurs. and Fri.

Do you have a strong stomach? Well, if you also enjoy comedy and magic, this may be your show. It can be a bit dark and gruesome in nature, however. Penn and Teller are Vegas legends, and they perform at the beautiful Rio resort, located right off the Strip.

This duo, with the notoriously smaller, silent Teller, and the larger, verbose Penn, love to perform grand illusions and also smaller, more unique tricks. They also love to show the audience how many of these illusions are performed, which is quite rare in the magic world. Please note that this show is often full of some blood (fake, of course), so if you are squeamish, this is not the show for you.

Music

The music scene in Vegas is always evolving. In recent years, big names like Celine Dion, Elton John, and Britney Spears have all taken up residency in this city. Living in Las Vegas and making a living has become big business, and we as visitors have been the beneficiaries of this popular new trend. New names come and go, and, much like the magic scene, in Vegas, the music scene is always getting better, as well.

Backstreet Boys : Larger than Life – Planet Hollywood

www.planethollywoodresort.com. 1.855.234.7469. 3667 Las Vegas Blvd. South. Tickets from $68. Nightly, 9 pm. Dark: Sun, Mon, and Tues.

With over 130 albums sold worldwide, the Backstreet Boys are the official top-selling and most successful boy band of all time. This powerhouse group has been entertaining audiences for 22 years, and they are making quite a splash at the Axis Theater at Planet Hollywood.

They come back for performances in June and July of 2017, and fans take note - this is a crowd pleaser, with the men singing their favorite songs, as well as many fan-favorites, as well. Very entertaining, these guys know how to perform, and the tickets are very affordable.

Boyz II Men – Mirage

www.mirage.com. 1.702.792.7777. 3400 Las Vegas Blvd. South. Tickets from $44. Nightly, Fri – Sun, 7:30 pm.

This threesome from Philly, who won four Grammys, are a consistent crowd-pleaser, and are currently performing at the Terry Fator Theater at the Mirage. This is truly a feel good show.

They not only sing their hit songs, but also add some humor and comedy to the show. Audience members consistently talk about how truly personable these guys are. Boyz II Men brings their R&B style of Motown Philly songs to the stage in a very pleasing way.

Britney Spears: Piece of Me – Planet Hollywood

www.planethollywoodresort.com. 1.855.234.7469. 3667 Las Vegas Blvd. South. Tickets from $79. Nightly, 9 pm. Dark: Sun, Mon, and Tues.

The Axis, inside Planet Hollywood, is a very hip, trendy theater that currently showcases some of music's biggest acts. Britney Spears, the pop diva, with over 100 million albums sold, performs here until December 31st, 2017, and her show is electric.

This 4,500-person theater houses the world's largest projection screen, and is roomy and a great venue. A feast for the senses, Britney flies across the stage, and entertains the audience with her dancing and iconic songs. If you are a Britney person, carve out some time for this show – you won't be disappointed.

Celine Dion – Caesar's Palace

www.caesarspalace.com. 1.855.234.7469. 3570 Las Vegas Blvd. South. Tickets from $55. Nightly, 7:30 pm. Dark: Mon & Thur.

The best-selling female artist of all time, Celine Dion has sold over 100 million records world-wide. A native of Canada, Dion is famous the world over, and her residency at the grand Colosseum theater at Caesar's has been widely hailed and lauded in Vegas by critics and visitors alike.

Celion struts around the stage in beautiful gowns, belting out her bevy of number-one hits. Dancers and visuals behind her add to her amazing lyrics and musical ability, and Dion genuinely seems like a lovely person, to boot.

Donny & Marie Osmond – Flamingo

www.flamingo.com. 1.702.733.3111. 3555 Las Vegas Blvd. South. Tickets from $95. Nightly, 7:30.

Two performers who are consistently very popular, particularly with older visitors to Las Vegas, Donny and Marie Osmond perform at a very nice theater inside the venerable Flamingo Resort. This brother and sister pair belt out a medley of their greatest hits, and also bring a solid blend of humor and dancing to the show, as well. This show will bring you back (if you were alive then) to their iconic 70's show.

There is a fun meet and greet option that guests can take advantage of. VIP seats, which are, of course, more expensive, include this option, or guests can pay $150 more to meet Donnie and Marie. A small photograph is included in this option.

Elton John : The Million Dollar Piano – Caesar's Palace

www.caesarspalace.com. 1.866.574.3851. 3570 Las Vegas Blvd. South. Tickets from $55. Days vary – call the theater directly or go online.

Yes, there is a piano onstage – a giant one! Is it worth a million dollars? Probably, because the thing is huge! This piano actually weighs 3,000 pounds, and is the centerpiece of this rollicking, amusing show.

Elton John has sold a whopping 250 million records, and is a legend, period. He makes this show what it is – very entertaining and exciting. He belts out his favorite tunes, and this show will certainly please any Elton lover. He is very pleasant, and a great showman, to boot, so if you are an Elton John fan, this is a great show to take in.

T-Mobile Arena – Las Vegas Strip

www.t-mobilearena.com. 1.888.929.7849. 3780 Las Vegas Blvd. South.

The vast T-Mobile Theater, right next to the MGM Grand, showcases some of music's biggest stars. The roster rotates from season to season, so be sure to check their website to see who's going to be in town when you visit. Notable musicians who will be performing here in the months to come include country great George Strait, Adam Lambert with Queen, Iron Maiden, and New Kids on the Block with Paula Abdul and Boyz II Men.

There are three very handy restaurants at the T-Mobile Arena, including Hollywood's famous eatery, Pink's Hot Dogs, and the place, which is relatively new, is a very nice place to enjoy a concert. The NHL's new Las Vegas team, the Golden Knights, will also play here in the months to come.

Variety

Cirque du Soleil

This very successful franchise has a major presence in the Las Vegas entertainment scene. Originally from Canada, the Cirque brand can be found in many American and international cities, including Orlando and Atlanta. Check out their official website, **www.cirquedusoleil.com** for more details and history.

Most people are familiar with this brand of entertainment, and now Las Vegas is alive with Cirque, with its' amazing acrobats and performers in these pulse-pounding shows. Currently, there are seven amazing Cirque shows. Prices generally start at $90 and up, with O, at the

Bellagio, generally being the most expensive option among the group. The theatres are exquisite, and Cirque's performers are amazingly talented performers.

*Ka – MGM Grand

www.mgmgrand.com. 1.702.891.7777. 3799 Las Vegas Blvd. South. Tickets from $78. 7 and 9:30 pm nightly. Dark: Thursday and Friday.

The original Las Vegas Cirque show, Ka still receives amazing reviews, and continues to pack in visitors almost every night. Set in a beautiful stage at the massive MGM Grand resort, Ka showcases Cirque at its' finest – acrobatics, music, and imagery all combine to envelop your senses.

This is definitely not a show that will bore you, unless this is just not your thing! Ka tells the story of twins that are on a mission to fulfill their shared destiny. Amazing aerial acrobatics, costumes, and pyrotechnics all add to the excitement of this journey.

Le Reve – The Dream - Wynn

www.wynnlasvegas.com. 1.702.770.7100. 3131 Las Vegas Blvd. South. Tickets from $135. Nightly, 7 and 9:30 pm. Dark: Wednesday and Thursday.

The title of this show is French for "the dream", and this show is very dreamlike, for sure. Situated in a stunning, round theater at the equally stunning Wynn resort, this show features many swimmers, many of whom dive off of very high platforms. This show has won the award for Best Production show for four straight years, which is unprecedented in Las Vegas.

The sheer amount of aerial acrobatics, swimmers, and dancers is amazing, and really serves to encompass the audience, stirring all of our senses simultaneously.

Michael Jackson ONE – Mandalay Bay

www.mandalaybay.com. 1.702.632.7580. 3950 Las Vegas Blvd. South. Tickets from $69. Nightly, 7 and 9:30 pm. Dark: Wednesday and Thursday.

If you are a fan of Cirque and the King of Pop, you simply can't go wrong here. Situated at Mandalay Bay's sumptuous theater, this show showcases a wide array of Michael Jackson's greatest hits, and the usual colorful images, spot-on acrobatics, and athleticism of a typical Vegas Cirque show.

More than 63 talented performers bring their talents to create a very unique show. Aerialists, acrobatics, and an amazing soundtrack all fuse together to make ONE, which is highly entertaining.

Mystere – Treasure Island

www.treasureisland.com. 1.800.392.1999. 3300 Las Vegas Blvd. South. Tickets from $49.50. Nightly, Sat – Wed, 7 pm & 9:30 pm.

A must-see for any Cirque fan, Mystere is French for "mystery", and this production is, indeed, very mysterious. 75 talented performers invade the stage with singing, dancing, acrobatics, and aerialists. Set in the beautiful Treasure Island resort, the theater is grand and fitting for a production like this.

The colorful costumes and amazing makeup only add to the drama and the comedy that is Mystere. This is a great first Cirque show to witness, as it introduces guests nicely to what Cirque is all about – mystery, agility, and drama.

O – Bellagio

www.bellagio.com. 1.702.693.7111. 3600 Las Vegas Blvd. South. Tickets from $100. Nightly, 7 and 9:30 pm. Dark: Monday and Tuesday.

The priciest of the group, O stands for "eau", which is French for water. As you might expect, a Cirque show at the stunning Bellagio does not disappoint. A massive, circular stage is the centerpiece for this show, and it's pretty ingenious.

O is known for its' blend of amazing, death-defying acrobatics, music, and colorful imagery that makes it a truly unique show. Of course, tons and tons of water is involved in this production, making it all the more unique and jaw-dropping.

The fact that it's located in the beautiful Bellagio, to us, only makes it an even better show. Spend some time wandering around this sumptuous resort after treating yourself to O.

The Beatles LOVE – Mirage

www.mirage.com. 1.702.791.7111. 3400 Las Vegas Blvd. South. Tickets from $100. Nightly, 7 and 9:30 pm. Dark: Tuesday and Wednesday.

If you are a fan of the Beatles, like we are, you will surely enjoy this well-produced show at the Mirage. Some travelers report that the musical arrangement is not the best, but Beatles fans   should at least be pleased with this Cirque rendition.

Iconic Beatles song after song is played, as scores of talented acrobats take the stage and strut their amazing feats of strength and agility. The powerful music, accompanied by the acrobatics and costumes, creates a very memorable show.

Zumanity – New York, New York

www.newyorknewyork.com. 1.702.740.6969. 3790 Las Vegas Blvd. South. Tickets from $67. Nightly, 7 and 9:30 pm. Dark: Wednesday and Thursday.

A way more adult version of Cirque du Soleil, this show is very risqué, and will not appeal to everyone, that is for sure. Sexuality is at the core of this Cirque show, and kids will need to skip this one. The usual Cirque feats of acrobatics, imagery, and bravery are all showcased here, but in this show, they are fused with scenes that evoke bondage, s & m, homosexuality.... you get the point, right?

This is not our cup of tea, personally, but many visitors love do love Zumanity, as it showcases the Cirque style in a very unique manner, to say the least. This is a show that truly pushes the limits of sexuality on stage.

Adult shows

The following two shows really stand out in the crowded Las Vegas entertainment scene for their adult-oriented content. Las Vegas, is of course, known for being sinful and a bit naughty, and the options for a show are no different. If you are seeking a truly titillating show, check out these three options.

Chippendales – Rio

www.riolasvegas.com. 1.702.777.2782. 3700 West Flamingo Rd., Las Vegas. Tickets from $54.99. Nightly, 8:30 and 10:30 pm.

The very word "Chippendales" is synonymous with male strippers that are hot and sexy! Yes, this show still exists at the Rio, and it is still thriving. These men are hunky, and many of them can also sing, and will serenade several lucky members of the audience during each performance.

Simply put, these hunks sing, strut, and strip each night to the delight of the audience members, mostly female, who pack in to see this show. Very popular with bachelorette parties, Chippendales is a fun time if you're in the mood for this sort of thing, of course.

Fantasy - Luxor

www.luxor.com. 1.800.557.7428. 3900 Las Vegas Blvd. Tickets from $49. Nightly, 10:30 pm.

You may have heard that Vegas has some topless revues, right? Grin! Well, Fantasy is a more upscale version of a really nice strip club. To be fair here, this show does feature a bevy of beautiful women who both dance and pole dance topless, and it also features a talented lead singer, as well as a comedian.

Surprisingly, many couples choose to come to Fantasy to experience the revue together. Why? Well, we're not quite sure why, but Fantasy routinely receives very high marks from guests and critics alike, having received many top awards for the best adult show in Vegas. Shows are held nightly at 10 pm, so be prepared to be a night owl for this one, although trust us, these beauties will definitely keep you awake!

Thunder from Down Under – Excalibur

www.excalibur.com. 1.702.597.7600. 3850 Las Vegas Blvd. South. Tickets from $63. Nightly, 9 pm. 11 pm also on Thursday through Sunday.

Yes, they are hunky. Yes, they are Australian. Yes, they are half-dressed on stage. OK – 'nuff said! This show, at the Excalibur, is still going strong, after many years in Vegas, and the ladies love it. OK, some men too, of course. These men are all sufficiently chiseled and can actually dance and move very well. They perform strip teases on stage and dress up in a variety of costumes that make the ladies (and men) go crazy! This revue, not surprisingly, is very popular with groups and bachelorette parties.

Yes, they also pull select women on stage, so come dressed to impress! Shows are held at 9pm nightly, and an 11 pm show is added on Fridays through Sundays, as well. Tickets generally start at $50 a person.

Variety Shows

Variety of shows have a bit of everything, and Las Vegas has a few amazing ones. If you are seeking singing, dancing, and more, these production shows are just the ticket. Check out the following two!

Terry Fator – The Voice of Entertainment

www.mirage.com. 1.800.963.9634. 3400 Las Vegas Blvd. South. Tickets from $75. Nightly, 7:30, Sunday-Thursday.

Terry Fator is a very talented performer, and to us, just seems like a really nice and likeable guy. He is a world-class ventriloquist (you just simply won't see this man's lips move!), singer, and celebrity impressionist. He works with puppets and a talented cast. Some of the celebrities he impersonates are Lady Gaga and Dean Martin.

Fator toiled in his craft for 20 years, doing everything from church shows to elementary schools, until 2007, when he burst onto the national scene on the popular show, America's Got Talent, winning the whole show and a million dollars in 2007.

He moved to Las Vegas immediately and a star was born at the Mirage. His show is critically acclaimed and award-winning, and guests love the humor and talent that Fator and his cast exude. This is consistently one of the top shows in Las Vegas, so book this one early!

V: The Ultimate Variety Show – Planet Hollywood

www.planethollywoodresort.com. 1.866.983.4279. 3663 Las Vegas Blvd. South (at Planet Hollywood's V Theater). Tickets from $49.99. Nightly, 7 and 9:30 pm.

A virtual hodgepodge of a show, V is a dream come true for the visitor that wants a bit of everything in a Las Vegas production show. Very talented magicians, comedians, aerialists, skaters, singers, jugglers, and dancers all perform in a medley of acts in this small theater inside the Planet Hollywood's Miracle Mile shops.

This show has won several major awards in Vegas for best production show, and it's easy to see why when you witness the talent and creativity that goes into V: The Ultimate Variety Show. Prices start at $49.99, which is a steal for a show of this caliber and acclaim.

Chapter 12 – Sports and Recreation

Las Vegas and sports do not exactly go together, but with its' brand new NHL team, and also the transfer of the NFL's Raiders to Vegas, this is quickly changing. Vegas is, of course, primarily a gambling and resort town, but there are plenty of fun recreational opportunities for girls and gals alike.

As always, make sure to visit our favorite travel website, **www.tripadvisor.com**, and see first-hand what recreational options abound. Here are some of our favorite picks when we need a change of pace in Sin City.

Baseball – Las Vegas 51's

www.milb.com. 1.702.943.7200. 850 Las Vegas Blvd. North, Las Vegas.

Many visitors have no clue that there is an actual baseball team that plays in Las Vegas, not too far from the Strip. The Las Vegas 51's, formerly the Las Vegas Stars, are named for the infamous Area 51 in Nevada, where aliens are a frequent sighting. They are the official minor league, triple-A team for the New York Mets.

Games take place at Cashman Field, a cozy ball park where you can get tickets for as cheap as $10 a person. A bevy of food and drinks are available for purchase as you watch the game. Minor league baseball games are a fun way to spend a few hours, as it is a laid-back atmosphere, and it's nice to see great athletes that are fighting to get to the majors, so they are very intense.

Golf

Yes, you are in the middle of a desert, but there are several amazing golf courses to choose from. One thing is clear, too – you don't really have to worry about rain when you decide to hit the links in Vegas!

The Wynn and the Baliahi golf courses are the two most well-known, and probably the best. Other fun recreational golfing places can be found, and provide the golf lover in your family a few hours away from the hustle and bustle of this twenty-four hour city.

Check out **www.lasvegasgolf.com** for all the information on the golf scene in Vegas. This is an informative website that will give you lots of specifics and pricing information on the burgeoning Las Vegas golf scene.

Make sure to wear your sunscreen and a hat and/or sunglasses when heading out to golf – remember that you are smack dab in the middle of the desert!

Balihai

www.balihai.com. 1.888.427.6678. 5160 Las Vegas Blvd. South.

A South seas-inspired golf course, Balihai is well-known in Vegas for its' beautiful and challenging course. Located behind the similarly-themed Mandalay Bay resort and offering panoramic views of this resort, Balihai offers golf lovers a fun afternoon in the sun. Make sure to wear your sunscreen and your sunglasses for this course!

Prices start at $170 for eighteen holes, and this facility offers golf equipment rentals, a fully-stocked pro-shop, and a bar, as well. A nice Polynesian-themed restaurant is onsite, as well, that overlooks the golf course. Balihai also offers stay and play packages at the Luxor, the Venetian and Encore, as well as the Mirage, which offers a set price for several nights at these hotels and includes golf outings, as well.

Wynn Las Vegas

www.wynnlasvegas.com. 1.702.770.4653. 3131 Las Vegas Blvd. South.

The Wynn Las Vegas golf course is known among golfers for its' beauty and the fact that it is very challenging. Located right behind the beautiful, gleaming Wynn resort, this golf course is a beauty and also, according to insiders, a tough but entertaining course to play. Prices for eighteen holes start at around $500, making this a very expensive day, but you can't really beat the scenery, with the amazing Wynn and Encore resorts gleaming right behind you.

Like most other golf courses in town, the Wynn offers a fully-stocked pro shop, club rentals, and also a bar to wet your whistle at the end, or beginning, of your 18 holes.

NFL – Raiders

www.nfl.com.

Football fans, get ready! The Oakland Raiders, a long-time fixture of the National Football League, are moving to Las Vegas. The move will take place either in the 2019 or 2020 season, depending on the completion of the amazing 1.9 billion-dollar Las Vegas Stadium. This brand-new arena will be located behind Mandalay Bay and the Luxor, and the NFL expects ticket sales to sky rocket. Finally, the NFL is coming to Las Vegas!

TopGolf

Top Golf is a fun concept in golfing, fusing golf with music, socializing, and swimming. This property, situated just behind the MGM Grand, features 18 climate-controlled hitting bays where you can play interactive games, two pools with VIP cabanas, 5 unique bars, a restaurant, a pro-shop, and also a concert venue for rent.

TopGolf is definitely not your father's golf course, that's for sure, and caters to a younger crowd, but all ages are welcome. The staff is very accommodating, and the prices are right, with prices starting at $30 a person. It is also a unique and fun way to spend a few hours, even if you're not a huge or experienced golfer.

Hockey

www.nhl.com/goldenknights

Yes, the NHL finally has descended upon Sin City. In 2018, the Las Vegas Golden Knights will commence play in Vegas, marking the first official professional sports team to take up residency in this city. Known for gambling and recreation, Las Vegas has really not focused on professional sports much, but this could be changing with the Golden Knights in town, and the fans are very excited, as many season tickets have already been sold!

They will play their games at the brand - new T-Mobile arena, a really nice venue situated between New York, New York and the Monte Carlo. Tickets will run between $15 and $440, so hockey lovers, eat your heart out!

Race Car Driving – The Richard Petty Driving Experience

www.drivepetty.com. 1.800.237.3889. 7000 North Las Vegas Hwy, Las Vegas.

As we covered in our thrills chapter, race car driving is an incredibly popular sport in America, and Richard Petty is an American racing legend. Petty owns and operates over 20 tracks in America, and the Las Vegas track is definitely one of the most well-known. This fun racetrack is revered in Vegas, and will give the racing lover in your party a fun few hours!

Prices start at $109, which gives you a ride-along experience with a professional driver, and prices extend up to $2699, which gives you an immersive experience driving a real Nascar car. Guests with a valid driving license have the opportunity here, hence, to drive a real car, which is a great adrenaline rush. The staff is gracious and attentive, and this can be a fun couple of hours, in a track only 15 miles from the Strip.

Walking the Strip & Downtown

Yes, this doesn't necessarily seem like exercising, but, trust us – once you are trudging along in the desert heat of Las Vegas, you will know very quickly that you are burning a lot of calories! One thing you will see very soon after arriving in this city is just how deceptively far one resort is from another. Just walking from Mandalay Bay, for example, which sits at the far southern end of the Strip, to the Monte Carlo, which is about a half-mile away, can take you up to an hour. You will want to explore each casino, and the shops and restaurants, and this takes awhile. A visitor can easily walk over 5 miles a day, just wandering around, exploring this fun town.

Your feet will definitely feel it after a day in Vegas, but it's a good tired, in our opinions. One of our favorite walks is from New York, New York to Caesar's Palace, and stopping to shop at both Bellagio, with its' upscale shops and sumptuous casino, and then continuing on to the Forum Shops. Make sure to stop and refuel along the way with a tasty meal or snack.

Exploring downtown can also be a good way to get in your daily exercise. Although the casinos here are much closer together, if you spend even a few hours exploring, you will burn a lot of calories and have fun doing so.

Chapter 13 - Nightlife in Las Vegas

The image of a pulsating nightlife is almost a symbol of Las Vegas. Rest assured, there are many nightclubs and lounges where you, provided you are at least 21 years of age, can party the night away! When many people think of Las Vegas, the typical Strip Club comes into mind, and, yes, there are dozens of those, but there are also many unique bars, nightclubs, and other watering holes. We have listed our best of the best!

Bars

Yes, there are a ton of bars in Sin City – are we shocked? Some are fun and exciting, and some are pretty typical bars that can be found in any city. We have chosen a few very popular ones to highlight, and to steer you in the right direction.

The Bar at Times Square

www.newyorknewyork.com. 1.702.740.6969. 3790 Las Vegas Blvd. South (inside New York, New York.) $10 cover charge after 7 pm.

A Vegas classic, The Bar at Times Square is located inside the exciting New York, New York resort. As you approach this bar, you may well feel like you are in the Big Apple, as this resort is a wonderful recreation of Manhattan. This bar is in the same vein, with New York City-style architecture and boisterous, festive performers. Open from 11 am to 2:30 am, this place appeals to those who want to let loose and see some great entertainment.

Each day and night, dueling piano players make the place come alive, and an enormous selection of drinks are available here, as well as a limited menu featuring burgers and other American fare. The bar is a fun place to spend a few hours, and to sing along to songs you love! Happy hour specials are available each day, as well.

Hogs and Heifers

www.hogsandheifers.com. 1.702.676.1457. 201 North 3rd Street, Las Vegas. No cover charge.

Attention, readers! If the sight of ladies' bras behind the bar and scantily-clad bar maidens frightens and/or offends you, please don't go to Hogs and Heifers. This is a very unique bar, to say the least, but a fun time can be had here is you know what you're in for. The sight of a long row of motorcycles out front sets the scene for what's inside this bar, that is for sure.

Bar maidens, wearing only a bra, dance on the top of the bar, as fiery bartenders shout out patrons' orders, and the whole scene is something out of a movie. Security is tight, so don't be worried if you see very large men securing the place. The atmosphere, however, is not hostile, but fun and festive, and very rowdy, as well. Hogs and Heifers is open from 12 pm until 4 am, so night owls will be very at home here.

Many say that this bar, which also has a location in New York City, was the inspiration for the Coyote Ugly series of bars, one of which is in Las Vegas, at New York, New York. In addition to the crazy bar scene, a menu with American pub fare is available here, as well as a bevy of drinks. Happy hour specials are available each day.

Peppermill's Fireside Lounge

www.peppermillslasvegas.com. 1.702.735.4177. 2985 Las Vegas Blvd. South, Las Vegas (between the Wynn and the Riviera).

Peppermill's is a Vegas classic, simply put. Numerous music videos and tv shows have been shot here. The vibe is cool and very Vegasy. Open 24 hours a day, this is a lounge, a bar, and also a thriving restaurant that serves three delicious meals a day.

Breakfast, which includes dozens of dishes, is available 24 hours a day. Peppermill's huge pancakes and omelets are very popular, and always baked fresh. The famous Peppermill burger is legendary in Vegas, and the nachos are amazing, as well.

The drink selection at the very hip bar is amazing, and local celebrities like Criss Angel have been known to pop into Peppermill's - yes, it's that cool. The location, between the Wynn and the Riviera, is not too out of the way, which is an added bonus to visiting Peppermill's.

The Piano Bar at Harrah's

www.caeasars.com. 1.702.369.5000. 3475 Las Vegas Blvd. South (inside Harrah's). Cover charge: varies based on day (roughly $15).

A rollicking piano bar, this spot is very similar to The Bar at Times Square, as it also features dueling piano players, rocking their hearts out. The talent here is amazing, and it's a fun place to sing along to your favorite songs while enjoying a great drink. A very popular place, the Piano Bar at Harrah's is one of those places that is fun to spend a few hours at, letting loose and enjoying the talented performers.

Karaoke is also featured here, as well as a full bar with a wide selection of drinks. Open until 1 am, this bar is a winner in the Las Vegas nightlife scene.

Ri Ra Irish Pub – Mandalay Bay

www.rira.com/las-vegas. 1.877.632.7700. 3930 Las Vegas Blvd. South. (at The Shops at Mandalay Place.) No cover charge.

A somewhat dark, atmospheric Irish pub, Ri Ra is a chain that can be found in other major cities. The menu includes both Irish and American dishes, and popular items include the Guinness BBQ burger and a variety of wings. A wide selection of drinks and Irish beers are available, and a fun feature of Ri Ra is a daily afternoon tea, which consists of finger sandwiches, freshly baked scones, desserts, and delicious tea. This afternoon tea service in a bar is the first of its' kind that we've ever seen in Vegas.

Happy hour specials are also available, from 11 am to 4 pm. Ri Ra also serves a delicious Irish-style breakfast, so be sure to check it out for a great way to start your day in Las Vegas. Ri Ra is a very dark, atmospheric pub, and feels very "Irishy" – is that a word?

Nightclubs

Attention, younger visitors to Vegas – the nightclub scene is thriving, and always adding new and unusual clubs. If a loud, throbbing dance floor and a long bar is your thing, you are in the right place! Almost every hotel has a nightspot, and the following nightclubs are good bets for those who enjoy this type of nocturnal activity.

Chateau Nighclub and Restaurant – Paris Las Vegas

www.parislasvegas.com. 1.877.796.2096. 3655 Las Vegas Blvd. South. Cover charge: $30: women. $20: men.

Chateau Nightclub and Restaurant is a new fixture on Paris' nightlife scene, and like the resort itself, this place is also very upscale and refined. Take note - this is not the Palms, people! A giant marble fireplace is the showpiece, as visitors gather around and drink a libation as they admire the amazing views of the Bellagio fountains across the street.

A thriving bar and dance floor round out the amenities here at Chateau, which, incidentally, means "house" in French. The clientele in this club is a bit more upscale and a bit older than other Vegas clubs. Note that this club is only open on Wednesday, Friday, and Saturday, so plan accordingly.

Diablo's Cantina – Monte Carlo

www.montecarlo.com. 1.702.730.7777. 3770 Las Vegas Blvd. South. No cover charge.

A rocking spot right on the Las Vegas Strip, Diablo's Cantina is also a trendy Mexican restaurant with amazing cuisine. An indoor/outdoor restaurant and nightclub, Diablo's, which means devil's in Spanish, by the way, is a unique way to enjoy a dinner and a drink. Ideally located center strip at the Monte Carlo, this place is very easy to get to.

Live DJ's spin hit tunes and a fully-stocked bar accompany the full-service Mexican menu. Dishes like nachos, tacos, hot wings, and their traditional baked queso fundido are all crowd pleasers here. Diablo's also specializes in a wide variety of tequila and frozen cocktails. Overall, this is a stunning 13,000 square-foot complex that affords great views of the Strip.

Hyde Lounge – Bellagio

www.hydebellagio.com. 1.702.693.8700. 3600 Las Vegas Blvd. South. Cover charge: $30: women. $20: men.

Bellagio is a very classy resort, and Hyde is no different than its' host resort. The Hyde Lounge is a 10,000 - square - foot indoor/outdoor nightspot that is open each night. Lavish chandeliers and towering glass doors adorn the Hyde, and make guests see very quickly that is not a rollicking nightspot.

The outdoor portion modeled after a Tuscan garden (fitting for this Italian-inspired resort), and it overlooks the fountains of Bellagio, and watching them dance each half-hour, to music, while clutching your favorite drink, is an enchanting way to end a wonderful day in Vegas.

Indoors, after 10pm, DJ's spin their music and Hyde also features frequent, live performances, as well. A wide variety of beverages and small plates from Bellagio's elegant Lago restaurant are available, as well. The Hyde is truly a unique experience, and also one that attracts young and old guests.

Marquee Nightclub and Dayclub – The Cosmopolitan.

www.cosmopolitanlasvegas.com. 1.702.333.9000. 3780 Las Vegas Blvd. South. Cover charge: $20 : women / $30 : men.

Marquee at the Cosmopolitan at City Center is a very hot spot in Vegas, and attracts mostly a younger clientele. The vibe is modern and hip, just what we would expect of a club located in the very modern and upscale Cosmopolitan. Marquee features both a day club, which includes their heated pool, and also a nightclub with a pulsating dance floor, huge bar, and rocking DJ's.

A 60,000 square foot rooftop patio here has amazing views of the Las Vegas Strip, but beware of the very expensive drinks! Review have always been very positive here, despite the pricey drinks. Marquee is open from 10 pm to 5 am, and is closed on Sunday, and Tuesdays to Thursdays. This is definitely a prime spot for night owls!

Tao Restaurant and Nightclub – Venetian

www.venetian.com. 1.702.414.1000. 3355 Las Vegas Blvd. South. Cover charge: Women: $10 / Men: $20.

Tao is both a chic restaurant and also a nightclub, and is located in the vibrant Venetian resort. Decked out in tones of striking shades of red and black, Tao is a happening spot for all ages, but mostly caters to the younger set, as you might guess. This club offers guests a massive dance floor, a full bar, as well as a fun and delicious Asian restaurant.

An impressive 20-foot statue of Buddha towers over guests, as well, really setting the scene for your experience at Two. We hear that the food is to die for, and items like the fried rice, sea bass, coconut shrimp, and sushi are all great options.

VooDoo Lounge – Rio

www.riolasvegas.com. 1.702.777.7777. 3700 West Flamingo Rd. Cover charge: Women: $20 / Men: $20.

An indoor/outdoor nightclub, the VooDoo lounge is famous in Las Vegas for its' amazing views and pulsating nightlife scene. Popular primarily with the twenty-something set, VooDoo also attracts many guests of all ages who stay at the Rio. The words "hip" and "cool" are definitely ones that can describe this place.

A massive spiraling staircase on the rooftop of the Rio is the stage for the outdoor portion of the VooDoo nightclub. The staircase leads you to jaw-dropping views of the glittering Strip and the mountains. A huge bar with a tasting menu can be found outside, and inside, guests can party the night away on the rocking dance floor with DJ's and a host of alcoholic drinks at the bar.

Strip Clubs

The movie, Showgirls, starring Elizabeth Berkeley, which many people consider just plain awful, really highlighted the thriving strip club scene in Las Vegas. No, the real strip clubs are not like this! There are a few really good ones, though, if this is your thing, of course! Las Vegas is a very hot spot to hold bachelor and bachelorette parties, due in large part to the wide variety of nightlife options, which includes, of course, the obligatory strip clubs. Check out the following two options, which are insanely popular in Vegas.

Sapphire

www.sapphirelasvegas.com. 1.702.869.0003. 3025 Sammy Davis Drive, Las Vegas. Cost: Free with complimentary limo service, and $22 without limo service. 10am-6pm is happy hour with ½ off drinks.

A topless club that is legendary in Las Vegas, Sapphire is located off the Strip and is a hotspot for those seeking beautiful women. A cool perk of going to Sapphire is that they offer complimentary limo service from any hotel, and this includes free admission. Another cool perk is that Sapphire has a pool and they feature pool parties in nice weather. Imagine that scene, right?

Note that every day, from 10 am to 6pm, Sapphire offers happy hour, where drinks are always half off. The club is open 24 hours a day, 365 days a year.

Sapphire does have a very defined dress code, so be aware when you're heading out. They request that no tank tops, open-toed shoes, jerseys, or sweatshirts be worn. VIP rooms are available for rent, and bachelor parties are popular here.

Spearmint Rhino Las Vegas

www.spearmintrhinolv.com. 1.702.796.3600. 3340 South Highland Drive, Las Vegas. Cost: Free with complimentary limo service, and $44 without limo. 6 am to 7 pm is happy hour, with drinks from $4.

Despite the weird and creepy name, Spearmint is a very good strip club, but it is more expensive than Sapphire. Like Sapphire, however, they offer free limo service from any hotel that includes admission, which can save you a lot of money! Happy hour runs from 10 am to 7 pm, with drinks from $4.

Spearmint features tons of seating areas, and some are intimate, and great for lap dances, which are $20 each. A special $100 VIP lap dance package can be purchased, and this includes 3 lap dances. Like Sapphire, this place is also open 24 hours a day, 365 days a year, so it's always a hopping nightspot and day spot, as well!

Chapter 14 - Getting Married in Las Vegas

Yes, we did it! Along with thousands of other couples each year, Las Vegas is one of the most popular places in the country to get married. Let's face it - it's fun, exciting, and your honeymoon can be built in, right? Plus, who can forget the many celebrity couples that got married here? Let's see – Britney and that guy, Michael Jordan, Richard Gere and Cindy Crawford, and the list goes on and on.

Many on-Strip chapels will be a more expensive option for couples, and, as a rule of thumb, the cheaper options are all off-Strip. We chose to get married at the Chapel at the Excalibur resort, and the experience was wonderful, stress-free, and not expensive! The options detailed below are not exhaustive, of course, but should guide you in the right direction if you want to get hitched in Sin City.

Hot Tip!

Make sure to know the basics before deciding to get married in Las Vegas. There is a mandatory $77 fee for your marriage license, and there is no blood test or waiting period needed. The marriage licenses can be obtained at the Clark County, located at 201 East Clark Ave, Las Vegas, 89101. The number is: 1.702.671.0600, and their website is: www.clarkcountynv.gov.

A Little White Chapel

www.alittlewhitechapel.com. 1.800.545.8111. 1301 Las Vegas Blvd. South. Price: Inexpensive.

Have you ever, for some strange reason, dreamed of a drive-through wedding? Well, you've come to the right place!

This iconic chapel, located off-Strip, with its' large gaudy sign out front has become a symbol of a brash Las Vegas wedding. This chapel is very popular, and has won awards on Tripadvisor for their gracious service, low prices, and efficiency and selection of wedding packages. Prices are very reasonable, starting in the mid $100's, so your budget can probably handle this one.

A Little White Chapel offers many different types of wedding and also vow renewal ceremonies. Guests can even choose a drive-through wedding, as we mentioned, which is not offered in many places in Vegas. An Elvis impersonator can also marry you and your spouse – does anything say Vegas like Elvis marrying you?

The Chapel at Bellagio

www.bellagio.com. 1.702.693.7111. 3600 Las Vegas Blvd. South. Price: Moderate to Expensive.

Like the Bellagio resort itself, the chapels here are nothing short of exquisite and stunning. A variety of packages are available here, and range from around $1500 all to way to $25,000! The more expensive packages include a two or three-night stay at the Bellagio for the newly married couple.

Vow renewal packages are also available, and these and the wedding ceremonies themselves can be held in front of the famed fountains in front of the Bellagio, creating a pretty spectacular and unique wedding venue. Very Vegasy, right?

The wedding coordinators here, we have heard, are nothing short of gracious, and patient in their wedding planning skills, creating a nice ambience in which to tie the knot.

The Chapel at Excalibur

www.excalibur.com. 1.800.811.4320. 3850 Las Vegas Blvd. South. Price: Inexpensive to moderate.

A Medieval themed wedding? This might sound regal, but, sorry, the two chapels at the Excalibur are not themed. Instead, the two chapels here are actually very sedate, with simple, elegant flower arrangements and nice, gracious staff members who will help you every step of the way.

We got married here in 2014, and the experience was wonderful and very stress free. We paid only $179 for the basic wedding package that included the ceremony with a wonderful pastor, and 6 wedding photos. More elaborate packages, of course, are available, and amenities of these packages include limo service, more photographs, and a DVD of your wedding ceremony.

The Chapel at Excalibur receives very positive reviews overall, so make sure you book here early! Vegas is a very popular place, after all, to get hitched, and this place is a jewel.

The Little Vegas Chapel

www.thelittlevegaschapel.com. 2207 Las Vegas Blvd. South. 1.702.385.5683. Price: Inexpensive.

A very popular chapel, The Little Vegas Chapel is similar to several other off-Strip chapels. A bit gaudy and very Vegas, this venue is a bit hit with visitors who want a real Vegas-feel wedding. This chapel also receives rave reviews on TripAdvisor.com, so you can trust that real people have great experiences here.

Guests can choose between a traditional wedding, vow renewal ceremony, or a more unique Elvis-impersonator wedding, where an Elvis lookalike will actually officiate your ceremony! What says Vegas wedding more that this – really? The Little Vegas Chapel is also very friendly to the LGBTQ community. Prices here start at around $199, so they should be able to fit into almost anyone's wedding budget.

The Chapel at Luxor

www.luxor.com. 1.866.458.8968. 2900 Las Vegas Blvd. South. Price: Moderate.

If you love the Luxor resort, as we do, and you also love being in total control of your wedding, then this may be the wedding venue for you! Getting married here is all about choices. Guests can choose to tie the know in a variety of venues at the Luxor, including at the Titanic exhibit (on a reproduction of epic stairs from the hit movie), at the LAX Nightclub, and our personal favorite – in front of the Luxor, standing in front of the giant Pyramid and Sphinx.

A bevy of wedding coordinators will meticulously work with couples to plan the perfect wedding, or vow renewal. Prices start in the low 200's, and are therefore affordable for most. Of course, if you opt for a more traditional wedding, that is also available here, at the Luxor, in one of their beautiful chapels.

The Chapel at Wynn

www.wynnlasvegas.com. 1.702.770.7100. 3131 Las Vegas Blvd. South. Cost: Moderate to Expensive.

Like the Wynn resort itself, which is simply beautiful, so too are the chapels at the Wynn. Yes, getting married here is not exactly cheap, but there is a nice range of packages to choose from. You can actually choose, if you have the bank account for it, of course, a wedding package that will set you back a whopping $29,900, which includes a 3-night stay in either a Wynn or Encore salon suite and a 3-hour session with a wedding photographer.

Cheaper wedding abound, however, with the least expensive option being a $1,790 wedding that has way fewer amenities, but still is a wonderful option for couples wanting to get married in an elegant setting.

Each chapel and wedding you choose has an opulent salon, as they call it, filled with lush, fresh flowers and very attentive wedding consultants. You can't go wrong at the Wynn if you want a tasteful wedding. The service is very professional, and the entire feel is very upscale but not snobby.

Chapter 15 - Side Trips from Las Vegas

Yes, we can admit it – we are Vegas addicts, and we never really used to never venture outside of Vegas. However, there are many fun and interesting options outside of the city limits that have made us change our mind about this. Lake Las Vegas, Hoover Dam, and the Grand Canyon are just three examples of amazing side trips that will probably make you forget about Sin City for a day. But, don't worry – coming back to the city is always fun!!

As always, our favorite website is **www.tripadvisor.com**., the world's largest travel website. Packed with information, (yes – we've said this before!), this website offers unbiased opinions from travelers just like you. We also appreciate the thousands of photos from travelers, as well as access to websites of the official hotels and attractions themselves.

Another valuable website is **www.vegas.com,** which offers detailed pricing and tour information. This will surely help you gather all those little details that go into your trip. Many fun tours can be booked on this helpful website. Their number is: **1.866.983.4279.**

Grand Canyon National Park

www.grandcanyon.com. 395 State Route, Grand Canyon, AZ 86023.

One of the most amazing sights in the entire world, and one of the great wonders of the Earth, the Grand Canyon is certainly a sight to behold. 5 million people visit the Canyon each year, and it was declared a national park by the US government in 1919. The Canyon is a mile deep, and covers a whopping million acres of land.

A popular day or overnight trip from Vegas, the Grand Canyon is on many visitors' bucket lists, and is a fun and educational day for the whole family.

Many people do not realize that the actual Grand Canyon is only 50 miles from Las Vegas! However, to drive there takes quite a while due to the Canyon's unique topography. Located in Grand Canyon, Arizona, the Grand Canyon is about a four-and-a-half-hour drive from Sin City to the popular South Rim area of the Canyon. The Canyon has three other sections: the West, North, and East sections, and each boasts hotels for visitors.

Many popular tours provide round-trip transportation to and from your hotel or a meeting spot in Las Vegas. Contact **www.grandcanyon.com**, **www.grayline.com, www.papillon.com,** or **www.vegas.com** for more information. Many of these tours are about 15 hours, and some include a stop at the Hoover Dam.

Fully-guided tours at the Canyon itself with an expert guide generally start from $85, and are a great way to see everything, and really learn a lot. Visitors can also upgrade and pay a bit more to experience the fun IMAX ride that transports guests through a virtual Grand Canyon.

The relatively new Skywalk attraction on the East Rim is now open, and a very popular addition to the whole Grand Canyon experience. The Skywalk itself is a glass semi-circle that allows visitors to walk out and look 4,000 feet below, and gaze at the stunning Grand Canyon. A shop located next to the Skywalk sells passes for this attraction, and also sells hot lunches, snacks, and cold drinks, as well as a bevy of fun souvenirs.

Fun for all ages, the Grand Canyon also boasts many souvenir shops and restaurants that cater to all ages. Check out the official website (above) to check out the many hotels that cater to overnight guests.

Hoover Dam

www.usbr.gov/lc/hooverdam. 1.702.494.2517. Henderson, NV.

Another natural wonder, the Hoover Dam is a bit more sedate than the gleaming Grand Canyon, but nonetheless manages to entertain over a million visitors each year. Built during the Depression, from 1931 until 1936, the Hoover Dam actually helped to build the city of Las Vegas itself, and was named after President Herbert Hoover.

Located in nearby Henderson, a 45-minute drive away, many hotels in Las Vegas were built largely to house the thousands of workers that built the Hoover Dam. Without the Dam itself, Las Vegas probably would have taken a lot longer to become the city it is today – a major tourist mecca.

Many people wonder what function the Hoover Dam plays for Nevada. Your authors did, as well! Well, the Hoover Dam is used primarily for several purposes: it provides power for nearby cities, it stores water that is derived from the nearby Lake Mead, and is also used for recreation purposes, as many boating enthusiasts enjoy this beautiful area.

Like the Grand Canyon, many people opt for a guided tour to really experience the Dam in all its' glory. Gray Line, which can easily be booked through www.tripdvisor.com, is a great option, and tours start at $55. Exploring the Dam is a very educational experience, and hence, not for everyone. It is, however, truly a feat of architecture engineering.

Lake Las Vegas

www.lakelasvegas.com. 1.866.322.3583.

Lake Las Vegas is a hidden gem for most Las Vegas visitors that actually visit this entertaining spot. Situated about 20 miles away from the Strip, and an easy day trip, this is an Italian-themed resort consisting of hotels, homes, shops, restaurants, and also a golf course. A recreation of Florence's gorgeous Ponte Vecchio is stunning, and the bright colors of Italy are on full display here.

Two prominent hotels, the Hilton Lake Las Vegas and the Westin Lake Las Vegas, are both fun to explore. The Montelago shopping arcade is full of luxury goods and also souvenirs, and Seasons Grocery is handy to stock up on items for a scenic picnic on the lake.

Several restaurants, along with condos and homes, surround this lake, and will all make you feel like you are strolling along in Italy. A very challenging, Jack Nicholas - designed golf course is also here, and is perfect for the golfer in your family.

Treat yourself to a slice of pizza or a cup of gelato as you take a break from the crowds and madness of Las Vegas at Lake Las Vegas. Explore their website (above) before visiting to get a better picture of what this colorful resort has to offer.

Chapter 16 – Safety & Security in Las Vegas

Staying safe in Las Vegas requires some knowledge of the laws, and also a little vigilance. It's a good idea to know about the city before you go, especially if you are coming from out of the country.

Las Vegas is a moderately safe city, overall, and a lot of the crime actually comes from visitors around the globe, so keep that in mind. Beware of petty crime, and also little things like even crossing the street - jaywalking is actually a hazard here, with the non-stop traffic and thousands upon thousands of visitors. The police, on occasion, will stop you for this offense, and people do die here each year due to jaywalking – so be careful and vigilant.

The hotels on the Strip are extremely safe due to the "eyes in the sky", which is code for the thousands of security cameras that watch visitors' every movement. The resorts are housing millions of dollars in gambling revenue, so security is paramount.

From the time you step into a hotel to the to the time you leave, you are as safe as can be. Do, of course, exercise normal precautions, as you would anywhere, however, especially in your hotel room.

Casinos

The legal gambling age in Nevada is 21 years old. There is a good chance that you will stopped and carded (asked for your ID) - we have, and then asked to leave if you are gambling underage. Often, casino personnel will walk around the casino to make sure that no underage guests are gambling. Make sure you always have a photo ID on you at all times, just in case.

Drinking Age

The legal drinking age in Nevada is 21 years old. Most bars and restaurants will strictly enforce this, so think twice against using a fake ID. Be sure to have your license or other picture ID on you at all times. If you are in a bar alone, or with friends, always watch your drink like a hawk.

Drug stores

A giant, souvenir-filled CVS is located smack dab in the center of the Strip, near Planet Hollywood, and not only has all the basic CVS items that are sold nationwide, but also a great collection of souvenirs. This place is massive, but note that prices are high. There is a handy Super Walmart in Las Vegas, right near Sam's Town, that has much better prices and a better selection of good, as well.

*CVS: There are over 15 CVS stores in Las Vegas alone. The most handy one for visitors is located near Planet Hollywood on Las Vegas Blvd. The address is: 3645 Las Vegas Blvd. South. Their number is : **1.702.474.4089.**

*Walmart: A Walmart Supercenter is located on Boulder Highway, near Sam's Town, and about 6 miles from the Strip. A free shuttle links guests to Sam's Town, departing from Harrah's. Walmart's address is: 5198 Boulder Hwy. Their number is : **1.702.434.5595.**

Hospitals

A very handy, well-respected hospital is the **Sunrise Hospital and Medical Center**, located on the east side of town, very close to the Strip. The hospital is located on Maryland Parkway, and its' number is: **1.702.731.8000**. The address is: **3186 S. Maryland Parkway**.

Police

As a general rule of thumb, always call 911 in case of an emergency. The Las Vegas police are very vigilant, and will respond promptly to any emergency. Be sure to know exactly where you are (ie room number/street address), because that's one of the first things they will ask you if you do have to make that call. If you happen to hang up on a dispatcher, they are required to call you back, so beware of that.

Weather

As you may be aware, Las Vegas is located in the Mojave desert, so the climate is always dry and usually always hot or at least fairly warm. When we say hot, we mean really, really hot! The average high in July is a whopping 105 degrees!

If you are not used to this weather, it can be quite a shock to experience 90-degree weather at ten o'clock at night – yes, that has happened to us on numerous times! The heat is very dry, averaging a low of 22% humidity, so it doesn't feel nearly as hot as the thermometer may indicate.

It can get cold, of course, in winter time and even in late fall, so be aware of the weather when you are packing for your trip. The average year-round high is roughly 70 degrees, so Las Vegas is pretty perfect if you don't mind hot, dry weather.

From October to March, we recommend taking at least one sweatshirt and/or a light jacket. In warmer months, make sure to take a good pair or two of sunglasses, and also sunscreen. Bathing suits are a must, as well, and always take your walking shoes. Getting a sunburn is very common here, and you will see plenty of your fellow visitors walking through the casino with a bright red face, because they neglected to put on enough sunscreen.

Printed in Great Britain
by Amazon

24404846R00091